The Lost Shrine of Liskeard

The Lost Shrine of Liskeard

Claire Riche

The Saint Austin Press
MMII

THE SAINT AUSTIN PRESS
296, Brockley Road
London, SE4 2RA

Telephone: +44 (0)20 8692 6009
Facsimile: +44 (0)20 8469 3609

Electronic mail: books@saintaustin.org
http://www.saintaustin.org

ISBN 1 901157 63 6

A catalogue record for this book is available from the British Library.

Printed by Newton Printing Ltd, London, UK. www.newtonprinting.com

An lyver fest didheurek ma a hevel kuntell kemmysk koynt ha kevrinek a geslammow ankoth. Byttegyns, yns i keslammow dhe wir, po an towl gwius kompleth a Dhyw? A vydh asverys Maria, Mamm Dyw, dh'y hen grerva dhe Bark an Arloedhes, yn Lyskerrys, po an Jowl, a wra ev tryghi er hy fynn, owth omdhiskwedhes der an nerthow drog a "Kerrid", dywes ankredorek ankevys nans yw hirnedh?

Dres dewgens blydhen, bythkweyth ny ankevi an Doktour Margaret Pollard gorholedh ankrysadow Maria leverys dhedhi yn Russek, 'Gorr vy dhe-dre!' An hwedhel ma, hwath ow tispletya hedhyw yn Kernow keltek a dheg an keth spyrys avel an henhwedhlow Arthurek ha'n Gral Sans. Yn surredi, hwedhel gwir yw hemma ha kovadhys gans onan a aswonni yn personek an "Peggy" Pollard skentel ha roasek dres eghenn. An awtour a vir war-tu an termyn a dheu rag 'an Grerva Gellys a Lyskerrys' ha mynnasow Maria Wynn a Gernow.

Philip Knight,
Cornish Bard

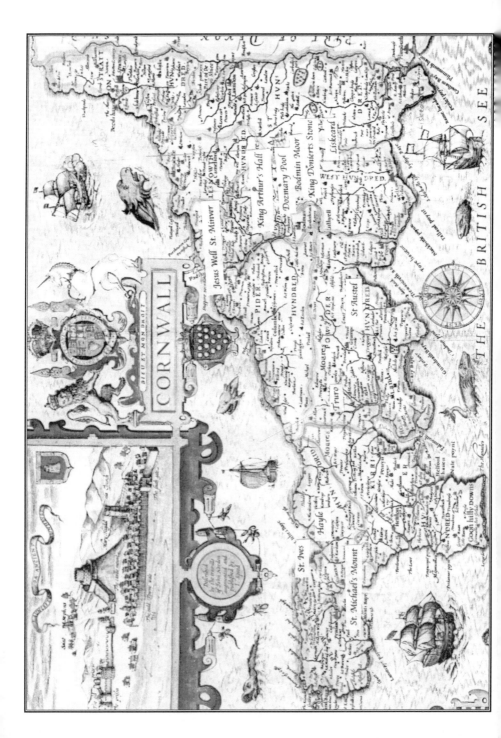

Contents

Dr Margaret (Peggy) Pollard

Introduction

In 1947 a book entitled 'Cornwall' was written by a Peggy Pollard and published by Paul Elek Publishers London. It began:

"Everybody knows everything about Cornwall already. It is the most overwritten tract of land under the sun. Ghosties, ghoulies, figgy'obhen, Frenchman's Creek, piskies and surf bathing at Newquay are what every schoolboy knows, as does he also (praise the Lord!) by now, that it is abomination to erect red roof here in the midst of traditional gray slate."

Since that time even more volumes have been written about Cornwall but none like this one. It is not a history book, although many will find fascinating historical snippets within its pages. It is not a theological treatise, although at times it details the theology of Peggy Pollard, whose work is quoted above. It is not a novel and yet on occasions reads as such. It is a book full of mysticism and interest, describing the discovery of part of Cornwall's long lost cultural and religious heritage, stretching back over two thousand years, which could well have great significance in the third millennium, not just for Cornwall but the whole of England and beyond.

The tale is told via original letters (all in my possession), stories, and thought provoking incidents, which took place during the years 1955 - 2001.

"*La Vierge à la Porcelaine*" painted by Margaret Pollard.

Chaptra Onan

(Chapter One)

Treylyans
Conversion

In every generation certain personalities stand out from the crowd and their passing leaves a never-to-be-forgotten mark. Some go down in history and others become the basis of legends. On 13th November 1996, the county of Cornwall, in the far West of England, lost a colourful character, Margaret Steuart Pollard PhD, who falls into the latter category.

She was born into the famous Gladstone family (of Gladstone Bag fame!) and had what many would call a privileged upbringing, but from her own accounts, her experiences at the hands of 'vicious nannies' are more likely to be called abusive, when set against modern day standards. However, she survived their onslaughts and ended up at Girton College Cambridge, studying Oriental Languages in the early 1920s. This was an unheard of subject at the time for a female. Not only did she study it, she became the first woman to get a double first in the subject.

Whilst at Girton, she developed, as well as her linguistic talents, her musical ones. She was playing the guitar there, long before it had become a popular student instrument, and told tales of how the maid (it seems in those days students had their own maids!) amazed freshers by informing them on arrival "No one must use that cupboard because Miss Gladstone keeps her 'goitre' in there!"

Margaret was before her time in many other ways too, being very concerned with preserving the environment for posterity.

Soon after coming down from Cambridge, she married a dashing naval officer, also a Cambridge Graduate, to whom she always referred by his surname "Pollard." This society wedding, which took place at St Margaret's Westminster, would seem to be putting her en route for a life of socialising and pleasure, but far from it! Very early in her adult life she began to turn from all forms of materialism. She began what today would be called the 'search for her soul'

She was already very familiar with the Indian gods, as her father always had a fascination for them. She felt a need to be 'at one' with Mother Earth and threw herself into what would now be called New Age practices.

As a Celt she was fascinated by their pre-Christian religion. She toyed with Druidism and as she said herself much later, "provoked the Almighty for 40 years in the wilderness" by becoming involved in anything as long as it was not established contemporary religion. She even dabbled in witchcraft and long after she had given up such practices, she amused herself by giving talks on the subject to women's groups and others. In her book "Cornwall" (Paul Elek Publishers 1947) she tells the story:

"I was lecturing to the Women's Institute on this subject, and said to them: "I will now show you a Scottish charm to raise the wind. Unfortunately it only applies in the old-fashioned sense of the phrase. You tie a knot in a handkerchief or scarf, and strike it hard on a stone or hard surface"...taking off my own scarf and tying a knot in it..... "saying these words:
'I knok this rag upon this stane
To raise the wind in the divellis name.
It shall not lye till I please again"

Now until this moment the evening had been dead calm and windless. As I spoke these words a sharp violent squall arose and almost deafened us. It subsided as suddenly. This mightily amused the audience, and naturally I took the credit; but the same thing happened at St. Just-in-Roseland some months later; and when it happened a third time I was sufficiently impressed to leave this act out of my lecture. Certainly I did not attempt any "horse and pellatis" stuff with a hemlock stalk."

In 1940 she wrote an irreverent pastiche on Cornish miracle plays, *Bewnans Alsaryn,* which won the prize that year in the bardic competition, which is held by *Gorsedh Kernow* (Cornish Gorseth). It was regarded as one of the finest blossomings in the Cornish revival. Written in verse, it runs with a marvellous beauty and fluidity, which is a joy to whosoever reads it. It features Alsaryn, who possesses a negative faith. He believes in neither God nor the devil, but goes his own way, which is what she would say she was doing at the time. In many ways Alsaryn could be her, though male and living in a different era.

Then one terrifying night in 1944, she narrowly escaped death by fire, but what affected her more was her sudden realisation that her whole life had been concerned with religions of the past. She was alive today, but where would she be after death? Had God, if there was one, saved her for a reason? If he had she must thank him - but how? She was not on speaking terms with him. She did not believe in him, but he had saved her. The only prayer she knew was the "Our Father", but she could not bring herself to say it in English. She, who had always been so confident in all situations, suddenly felt unworthy to speak the words, which she had heard and seen so often, but which had been meaningless to her.

She was a great linguist and spoke Russian fluently. She always explained her reasons for learning Russian as stemming "from the worst possible motives." She first began to study the language at a time, when she was convinced that the world would be overrun by Russia and that England would be occupied. She was determined that when that time came, she would be ready for them. She realised that there would be very few Russian speaking English people, so she would be at a great advantage. If it happened, she was not quite sure whether she would keep quiet about her knowledge, so as to be able to find out what was going on, or whether she would use it to wheedle herself into a place of power, whence she would be able to procure jobs for all her friends!

She knew the Lord's Prayer in Russian, so started to say it in that language over and over again - all night. By the next morning she knew she must seek out the Christian church. Coming from a background of 'establishment' as it were, she automatically approached the Church of England. The most well known C of E church in Truro (where she lived) was the cathedral, and that fitted in with her view of where the God she was seeking should live. It was very fortunate that the bishop at the time was Bishop Hunkin who, like herself, was very environmentally conscious. In those days most people had hardly heard the word 'environment', so as far as she was concerned, it was a sheer stroke of luck to be thrown into contact with him. He was chairman of the newly formed Cornish Branch of the Society for the Preservation of the Countryside in Rural England, a society very close to her heart. She became the bishop's secretary, which she said was great fun, because between them they had the society "stitched up".

Never being one to do things by halves, she also threw herself completely into being a committed member of the church and involved herself in every possible way with the work of Truro Cathedral, including embroidering kneelers, playing the organ, and running youth groups.

In the early 1950s Dr Margaret Pollard in her capacity as youth leader took a band of youngsters from the cathedral for a holiday in London. She found herself staying with them in a hotel opposite Brompton Oratory in Kensington. In tune with her idea of fun she suggested to her charges that it would be a lark to shock the bishop back home by attending a Catholic Mass (these were the days before ecumenism). So, crossing the busy main road, they mounted the steps to the great swing doors. What she found inside was to change her life for ever. The vast oratorium was filled with the most wonderful music. All around the church at many altars were priests, in ornate vestments, saying Mass. She felt the presence of God as never before in her life. It was as if time had been suspended, as she sat and watched and listened. When she came to, she realised that everyone was walking out. She knew she must find out what feast day it was, for surely only someone very special would have such a celebration. To her amazement the first few worshippers she asked did not know. "It is always like this" was the stock reply. At last she went up to an elderly gentleman still deep in prayer. She felt intuitively he must know, and he did.

" It's the feast of St Dominic," he replied.

"How can I find out more about him?" was her immediate reaction.

Find out about him she did, but it seemed as though St Dominic also had his eye on her, for within a week of returning home, Margaret met a Dominican priest. She had been visiting her mother in St. Ives when, walking past the Catholic church, she noticed that there was a talk on prayer that evening by a Fr Peter OP. She had no idea that OP stood for 'Order of Preachers' (commonly called the 'Dominicans'), but felt she would like to attend. She was enthralled by the speaker, who told the assembled group that the following Saturday he would be leading a pilgrimage to Fatima, a shrine of Our Lady in Portugal. Immediately the talk was over, she made herself known to this priest, who it turned out was only in Cornwall for a few days. She told him that as a result of what she had heard that evening she would "move hell and high water" to visit Fatima. He responded by assuring her that such drastic measures would be unnecessary, and suggested she join his crowd the following week. She cancelled all arrangements in order to travel with his pilgrimage group, and consequently less than two weeks after that memorable visit to Brompton Oratory she found herself being introduced to the rosary and preparing to be received into the Catholic Church. Her ardour for Our Blessed Lady and her beloved Son grew into a relationship so deep as to be incomprehensible to most of us.

One of Margaret Pollard's great disappointments on leaving the Church of England was having to swap worshipping and playing the organ in beautiful Truro Cathedral for a tiny hut-like Catholic church on the edge of town. It was a far cry from the sumptuous Brompton Oratory, where she had first been introduced to the Real Presence but, as she said, "Christ was born in a stable so I must go where He is." She realised, although she had not known it at the time, that it had been Bishop Hunkin she had found in the cathedral, not God; at least not the personal yet mystic God her soul had been yearning for all her life. She suddenly saw the Church of England, full of well meaning people in radio contact with God, but never being able to experience the full wonder and excitement of God still working and living in the world today. The following years saw her becoming as involved in the Catholic Church as she had been at the Cathedral. She ran the catechism classes, teaching the children exciting Bible stories (at that time rare in the Catholic Church), but now she taught them from a completely different perspective, as part of revealed truth. She took as many children as she could on visits to shrines, such as Fatima, Lourdes, Walsingham and Aylesford, enthusing them with her own love for the Blessed Virgin and the Eucharist.

Then on 2nd November 1955, as Margaret Pollard sat in her room at home in Pydar Street, Truro, Cornwall, she noticed a woman sitting in her arm chair.

"She was dressed in a variety of shades of blue, full flowing draperies and she wore a tiara-shaped crown with projecting rays that appeared to be jewelled with dull opaque stones like pearls and opals. She had dark hair and she began to speak. She spoke in Russian 'You have been a good cab horse to bring others to me. Now I want a ride myself. Lanherne is not enough for Cornwall. I want to come back to Liskeard.' " (Margaret Pollard's own words recorded soon after the event).

Margaret did not know quite what to make of this encounter. She knew she was not asleep, so could not be dreaming, but she was sceptical by nature, so she said to the lady, whom as she said later she took to be an apparition of the Virgin Mary:
" If you are who you seem to be, I need some sort of proof that you are who you are. Visions are two a penny and anyone to whom I mention this will think I am cracked, so before I stick my neck out for you, I ask you to stay there long enough for me to make a sketch of you. Then tomorrow I'll start painting a picture based on that sketch. I'll submit it to the Paris Salon, and if it is hung, which is most unlikely, I will accept that you are genuine and try to do something about your request."

The lady smiled and nodded her head. Margaret picked up an old envelope, which was the nearest thing to hand, and quickly started to draw. On completion of this self appointed task, she looked down, and then back up to the lady, but she had gone.

The next morning Margaret Pollard set to work painting her picture. It was based on what she had seen, but was not a true portrayal of the apparition.

She painted Jesus on Mary's lap whereas the child had not been present the previous day. Instead of her old arm chair she painted Our Lady seated in a dark cavern with her feet in water and in the child Jesus's hands she placed a cowrie shell. She entitled the painting (a water colour) *"La Vierge à la Porcelaine"*. Though many find it strange that she should paint a picture so different in form from the alleged vision, she always took great pains to explain that the painting was always meant to be 'a painting of Our Lady', not any particular representation and certainly not to explain her vision to anyone. "After all," she said, "It was I who suggested the painting for my own, and possibly Our Lady's, benefit, as a proof that I had been given the mission. I always liked to see Mary painted as a Madonna and Child, so that is how I portrayed her, and my old armchair would hardly have made a very good setting, so although I drew the face and clothes as I had sketched them on the envelope, the rest was pure artist's imagination."

She had never submitted a painting to any exhibition in her life and had no idea how to go about, it, but having told Our Lady that she wanted it hung in the Paris Salon, she knew what she must do. She packed it up and sent it off, enclosing a short note, saying something to the effect that she thought they might be interested in hanging it in an exhibition.

She had shown the painting to no-one before despatch. Nor did she even mention it, or the 'vision' to anyone until early 1956, apart from her spiritual director, Fr Esmond and he advised her to notify Bishop Cyril Restieaux, of Plymouth. This she did after first speaking to Fr Hackett, the parish priest at Liskeard.

In April she received a letter informing her that the picture would be hung in the Paris Salon summer exhibition. It is true that prior to this, her curiosity had overcome her and she had made enquiries as to whether there were any remains of a previous shrine in the Liskeard area. Also several events had happened, which she took to be further indications that Our Lady was proving that she had not been a figment of the imagination. However, Margaret Pollard's final belief that Our Lady, without a shred of doubt, had given her a mission was the acceptance letter from the Paris Salon. She had promised she would try and fulfil Our Lady's wish, if the picture were hung. Our Lady had kept her part of the bargain and now she must set about keeping hers.

It was not until late 1956 that the picture was returned and the question then was what to do with it. For some time it hung on the wall of Dr Pollard's home in Truro. It was pointed out to the few people, who were by then privy to the information concerning its significance. Apart from explaining that it was a picture based on the vision she thought she saw, rather than being a representation of what she saw, she gave no further explanation.

One of those given the inside story was the then Lady St Levan of St Michael's Mount. She was a Catholic, very active in the Catholic Women's League and organised religious summer camps for Catholic children at non-Catholic schools. Dr Pollard was also involved in this, so the two often met. On seeing the picture 'La Vierge à la Porcelaine' Lady St Levan fell in love with it. Back home at The Mount that night, she mentioned the painting to her husband Lord St Levan. As she had a birthday coming up, he asked her whether she would like him to purchase it for her as a birthday present. She was delighted at the idea and this he did for the price of £30. The money was immediately added to the shrine fund, which had been opened by then.

Lady St Levan's new acquisition was hung in her private chapel on St Michael's Mount, until she moved to the mainland in the late 1980s and took it with her. She once told the story of how on an occasion when Queen Elizabeth the Queen Mother was staying with her, the Queen stopped in front of 'La Vierge à la Porcelaine' and asked about its history. Lady St Levan hedged her bets and decided to reply, "It was painted by a friend who had a very vivid dream." The Queen was reported to have said, "I think you mean a vision."

Another occasion, when the painting was erroneously described as being the result of a dream, was in the early 1980s when Dr Pollard was co-writing a book, 'Our Lady of the Portal' for Truro Catholic Church. The painting was featured in the front of the book, but Faith Godbeer, the other co-author, was not prepared to put her name to anything, which declared a vision had occurred, so Dr Pollard was happy to allow it to be called a dream. Although she had absolutely no doubts in her own mind, that she had not been asleep, so could not have been dreaming, as far as she was concerned, a request had been made of her personally. The painting had been her own bargain with Our Lady, so there was no necessity for others to hear the history behind it. Faith Godbeer also wrote an interpretation of the picture in the book, saying the picture **"shows Our Lady seated at the entrance of a cave, and the child holding a large shell, representing pilgrimage. It links land, sea, and the devotion to the Portal, with the ancient and modern pilgrimages across Cornwall."**

When questioned about this interpretation in 1990, some 35 years after painting it, Dr Pollard was adamant, that this was merely a figment of Faith's imagination. It was not a pilgrimage shell. She explained in a letter:

"I exhibited under the title of La Vierge à la Porcelaine (cowrie)....It was my own personal thing. For the cowrie shell is a very beautiful ornament but no use whatever till it has died, been battered about by the ocean and cast up empty on the beach. While it lives it is dirty, slimy, smelly and no good to man or beast. It has to die and be painfully purified and then it is immortal. So I thought this is a model of the soul so put it in the Child Jesus's hands, because that was what I aimed to do myself and so it worked out because I am attached to nothing and nobody and as a result I can be useful. The cavern and river were not what I saw but I thought they seemed suitable and I was very keen just then on dark backgrounds done with my thumb; It was a shallow vein and soon worked out. But the figure was as I saw it. And I remember her name for me "IZVOZCHICHYA LOSHADKA", little cab horse. Not

likely I'd made that up!"

Lady St Levan died in 1995 and, although the whereabouts of the picture remained a mystery for some time, it is still in private hands and will probably be donated to the Catholic Church, if and when a permanent shrine to Our Lady is restored in Liskeard.

Dr Pollard herself never wrote or gave an oral interpretation of her painting (other than that quoted above), but since Lady St Levan's death it has been seen by a wider audience and suddenly it has come alive, with viewers seeing into it far more than Dr Pollard would ever have read. It is almost certain that, were Dr Pollard alive today, she would merely reiterate her original observations, and say that any interpretations are individual to the beholder and that they were not in her mind at the time of painting. This being so, some of the very obvious nuances such as a lamb and dove to be seen in the child's clothing are remarkable indeed.

As interpretations came thick and fast, once the painting was available to a wider, although still restricted, public, an approach was made to Sr Wendy Beckett, the Notre Dame sister living at the Carmelite Monastery in Norfolk. She became well known in the media in the 90s as an art commentator, but her reply in a letter was: "Maybe the hidden meanings in the picture are meant to be discovered by the prayerful gaze of each person, and not to be explained".

Above: The oldest part of Ladye Park House

Below: The stream flowing into the baptistry

Chaptra Dew

(Chapter Two)
MENYA DOMOI-**Gorr vy dhre-dre**
MENYA DOMOI - Take Me Home

In spite of having had told 'the lady' that she needed proof before she did anything drastic, which to her meant risking being thought mad, Dr Pollard could not but feel curious about the request which seemed to have been made. She had a copy of a map 'Shrines of England" by Martin Gillett on which a shrine of Our Lady of the Park Liskeard was marked, as no longer in existence. This was, she decided, a good starting point, so she found the name and address of the parish priest of Liskeard and wrote to him asking whether he had any information about the ancient shrine and its whereabouts. She gave no reason other than her interest in restoring it from a historical point of view. After some delay, he replied saying there were quite a few remains, but it was in non-Catholic hands, and while he was glad to hear of her interest, he did not believe there was any chance of restoring it. However, he thought he could probably arrange for her to view the place sometime.

It so happened that she was going 'up country' (i.e. to London) on 17th November for a few days. It must be remembered that, amazing though it may seem, not only was a trip to London still a major event for most Cornish people in 1955, the majority of people travelled by train rather than by car, telephones were not universally used, and there was only one class of post which not only always reached its destination the next day, it usually arrived the same day anywhere in Cornwall when posted there early enough in the morning. Thus no-one ever considered the possibility that a letter might not arrive, or even be delayed. Margaret Pollard was no exception. She posted a letter to Fr Hackett, the parish priest of Liskeard, saying that she would call on him on her way back from London on 21st to introduce herself to him and, if at all possible, visit the shrine site. She was not worried that she had not received his reply before leaving for her journey. However, she had overlooked the fact that even priests have holidays. Fr Hackett did not receive the letter because he was out of town for a few days.

On the night of the 16/17th November, the eve of her trip to London, Dr Pollard had another strange experience. She was unable to sleep as she was kept awake by a voice saying "MENYA DOMOI" which is the Russian for "Take me home." She found it very difficult to explain the voice afterwards. She said that at first she definitely felt it came from a person in the room. When she realised there was no one there, she found it difficult to work out where the voice was coming from. She got up from her bed and wrote the words in a note book. Unlike a radio, which comes from one point in the room, this seemed to be all around her and yet it was not a boomingly loud sound. Eventually she came to the conclusion that the voice was within her and she could only take it to be Our Lady speaking. This increased her resolve to investigate Liskeard further. Eventually she fell into a restless sleep, hearing the words whenever she was conscious. When morning finally came, the voice had stopped but the words she had written the previous night were plainly before her, proving without doubt that it had not been a dream.

Her business in London completed, Dr Pollard returned to Cornwall on 21st November, stopping off at Liskeard as planned. Finding the parish priest absent, she approached a Mr Volk, whose wife was cleaning the church at the time, and asked whether he knew anything about the remains of a pre-reformation shrine. He replied immediately that he knew it well and would escort her there if she wished, as it was only about ten minutes walk from the town.

This delighted Dr Pollard and they set off along West Road. Suddenly they turned into a rough woodland path, which Mr Volk explained was still called the 'Mass Path,' obviously a hang over from the days, when it would have been used regularly by locals on their way to Mass or by countless pilgrims visiting the shrine. The path was steep and winding with high hedges on either side. It was like stepping into something out of the fairy tale, 'Hansel and Gretel'. Being Autumn, it was ankle deep in leaves and Mr Volk, who was far from young, fell down twice, but this did not daunt his enthusiasm to show this stranger a place that noticeably fascinated him too. At last they emerged from the dark path on to a small lane, and directly opposite was another small path leading to a very old looking wooden gate marked 'LADYE PARK.'

The Mass Path had been like something out of 'Hansel and Gretel', but the sight now before their eyes could have been straight out of 'The Secret Garden' and behind the overgrown bushes and trees one could just see an 18th or 19th century farmhouse.

"Here it is," exclaimed Mr Volk as he pushed open the little gate and they stepped onto a stone bridge crossing a small stream. The owner's young grandson, Anthony Kelly, happened to be standing by the front door and he willingly showed them round. Dr Pollard's own description of that first visit was:

"The shrine site consists of an orchard (mentioned in ancient records) a small plain vaulted building under a grassy mound, overgrown with laurel bushes - perhaps a baptistery, at the edge of a pool. There is also a pretty well, but this is not part of the shrine. The lower storey of the chapel is built into the farmhouse, and there is a fine window with a dripstone, an arched gateway, a bricked-up arched doorway and two trefoil-headed loopholes. This was most exciting, and Mr Volk was as excited as I was."

On returning home to Truro, Margaret Pollard found to her amazement an unexpected legacy amounting to £600. Though this may not seem large by present day standards, in 1955 it represented more than a teacher's salary, so it was a sizeable sum. No word had yet arrived about the painting 'La Vierge à la Porcelaine", but with this legacy it seemed Our Lady would pay her own way home. This and her experiences that day in Liskeard were fast leading Dr Pollard to the conclusion that she was already receiving the proof she needed to continue with this mission. She immediately wrote to her spiritual director Fr Esmond Kilmeck, OP, of Malta, and told him the whole story.

Fr Esmond replied by return of post. He believed the story implicitly and stated that he felt the Bishop of Plymouth should be informed immediately. Dr Pollard was not sure. She felt that as the former shrine was on Fr Hackett's 'patch', she should at least tell him first and see what he thought. She therefore decided to make another appointment to see Fr Hackett when he returned from holiday and did this the following week. She took the £600 legacy cheque with her, with the express purpose of handing it over for use in case the shrine could ever be restored, and she told him the story. He listened politely, although without any enthusiasm. He did not believe anything could be done to restore the shrine, but when she produced the cheque and he saw the size of it, he immediately accepted that the bishop should be informed. He agreed to keep the money for her expressed purpose, and that he would make some enquiries, but he still felt the mission to re-open it was near impossible.

Derivys yw dhe'n Epskop
The Bishop is informed

Although aware that the Catholic Church does not easily accept 'visions', Dr Pollard decided in the light of the advice from both Fr Esmond and Fr Hackett to write to the bishop stating exactly what had taken place so far. "After all,' she thought "Our Lady can still get out of it because I haven't yet heard anything about the painting."

She was pleasantly surprised therefore to get a letter back from the bishop on 20th January showing he was both 'interested and encouraging' *(Dr Pollard's own notes)* and he asked to be kept informed of any developments. This was more than she could have hoped for and felt Our Lady must have had a hand in it.

True to his word Fr Hackett made enquiries locally. He paid a visit to Mr Kelly who lived at Ladye Park and discovered that the land on which the shrine stood was on lease to the farmer, not owned by him, as originally assumed. However, Mr Kelly mentioned that he intended making an offer for the land at some point in the future, and he stated that when he acquired it, he would have no objection to selling a part of the ground for the restored shrine. Fr Hackett relayed this information to Dr Pollard, who felt it sounded most hopeful, albeit an indefinite and far distant proposition.

In February 1956 Dr Pollard went down with measles. At a time before measles vaccinations this was regarded as a very infectious disease, and serious for an adult, so she was shipped off to Truro Isolation Hospital. Whilst there she had an irresistible urge to tell the whole story to a fellow parishioner, Gladys Riche. There was no reason why she should inform her rather than anyone else, or indeed at all. They were merely church acquaintances not personal friends, but she felt so strongly she should notify her, that she wrote a letter, which Gladys received on 7th March 1956. It was formally addressed as the modern fashion of using Christian names for all and sundry had not yet become established.

The Isolation Hospital
Truro

Dear Mrs. Riche,

"..... now I think I will tell you the great story because you are one of the few fanatical Catholics in Truro who really mean business and believe in the rosary. So you deserve to know.

Well, in November I saw an apparition of Our Lady who instructed me to set about restoring her old shrine at Liskeard. I made a note of the date, and wrote to Fr Hackett, the priest, asking if there remained any traces of the pre-Reformation shrine of Our Lady. He wrote back, very pleased to know someone was interested, said there was a well and a baptistery and part of a chapel, owned by a non-Catholic but friendly farmer.

I went and inspected it - then found out its history from a Protestant friend who has the old parochial records. It was going very strong. It lies in a beautiful valley and you get to it down a steep path called THE MASS PATH.

When I got home I found a surprise sum of £600 waiting for me which put the matter beyond doubt. I told my friend Fr Esmond O.P. Provincial of Malta. He took the story seriously and said the bishop must be told at once. It would be a grave error not to. So I told Fr Hackett the whole story and said should I tell the bishop. (Possibly the most impressive miracle of all was Fr Hackett's gradual progress from polite defeatism to keen enthusiasm.) He said yes certainly. So then I wrote to the bishop who wrote back at once saying he was getting in touch with Fr Hackett. The next development was Fr Hackett saw the farmer and found the site was owned by a family in Australia. He wishes to buy when his lease is up, and will raise no objection to the shrine being built.

Fr Hackett is already planning the layout of the shrine and says the bishop is very interested and has asked to be told of all developments. His last letter seems to imply that we may not have to wait long. The shrine consisted of a Holy well, a baptistery, a chapel and half and acre of orchard with a stream. Half the chapel is built into the farm-house. Fine old archway, dripstone windows, loopholes. The well is filled with an electric pump. The farm incidentally is called Lady Park.

Now this shrine is going to be dynamite. It'll be a tremendous focus for the West. Lanherne is too out of the way and it never was an official shrine. It (Lady Park) will probably be visible from the railway. It's about one mile out of Liskeard. You see I might have made all this up but there are two things that verify it a) the money b) the change in Fr Hackett's outlook. Follow a convoy of Blessings...schools among them of course....EXPECT MIRACLES

Yours (don't tell anyone else though)

M.S.P

What went through Gladys's mind on receiving the letter will never be known, but she replied on a postcard:

"and so Our Lady is about to reclaim part of her dowry. When the Spring flowers are in full bloom, may we go together and say the

Rosary at the site of the future shrine?"

Dr Pollard duly recovered from her measles ordeal and life returned to normal, but her 'mission' was still always at the back of her mind. She began to read up everything she could about Liskeard, a town she had known hitherto only as a railway station on the way to London, but now her interest was insatiable. She became very excited on 27th March 1956 when she discovered Our Lady's fleur-de-lys in Liskeard's borough seal. This appeared to be even greater proof that Liskeard had once been a great centre of devotion to Mary. During later research she decided that the fleur de Lys, in fact probably represented Kerrid's lily; Kerrid being a pre-Christian goddess of love and eternal youth whose emblem was a lily.

In ancient times, she discovered, Liskeard had been a centre of devotion to her and she was convinced that the very name 'Liskeard' was a derivative of '*Lys Kerrid*,' Cornish for "Court of Kerrid". It is not known what sources Dr Pollard used for her research in 1955, but one of the most authoritative place-name experts for Cornwall today is Oliver J Padel, formerly "Place-Names Research Fellow at the Institute of Cornish Studies (University of Exeter) at Redruth" in the late eighties. His entry for Liskeard in his "Popular Dictionary of Cornish Place Names" reads:

"*Lys Cerruyt c 1010,   Liscarret 1086, Lyskerres 1298. Probably Court of Kerwyd*", *but* there is no mention of *Kerwyd* being one and the same as *Kerrid*.

With the coming of Christianity it was very easy for the local people to transfer their love of Kerrid to Mary for it was almost as though God had planted a knowledge of Mary in their hearts without their knowing. Kerrid was definitely not Mary, but there were many similarities, which could be drawn, making it easier for people to make the transfer from many gods to a three in one god, and a human who had a unique place having become the Mother of God.

The date set for Gladys Riche's visit to Ladye Park with Peggy Pollard, as she was now known to friends, was 15th April, but three days earlier, on the 12th, Peggy had the chance offer of a lift to

Liskeard with two Anglican friends, Trevor Furze and David Clarke. She took it immediately, taking with her a miraculous medal at the suggestion of Fr Esmond in Malta. He had told her, in a letter a few days previously, that the Dominican nuns of the Perpetual Rosary in Buffalo New York were praying for Ladye Park as a special intention, and they were great believers in 'staking one's claim' by dropping a medal. She therefore visited the shrine site and did just this, although she confessed afterwards that she could not help wondering whether this constituted taking unfair advantage.

The morning of 15th April dawned sunny and warm, a typical English Spring Sunday. Coincidentally it was also Gladys's birthday. When her husband Sydney asked her a week or so previously, whether there was anything special she would like for her birthday she had replied, "Yes I'd like to borrow the car to go somewhere." At first he thought she meant that she planned to go on an outing with the family, but when he realised that she was going somewhere on her own he found it a little strange, and he was slightly perplexed, to say the least. The car was very much a family vehicle not belonging to anyone in particular. If one wanted it, one usually checked that no-one else needed it that day or at that time, marked up on the calendar where one was going, and that was that: the car was reserved. However, on this occasion nothing was recorded, but after Mass which the family attended together, Gladys declared that she was off and her eldest daughter, Ann, would be accompanying her. Ann was 20 yrs old at the time, so it was no surprise that she did not wish to inform the family where she was going, but Sydney could still not understand why his wife should keep the destination a secret from him. However, he was a good natured fellow, and waved them off, hoping they would have a good day.

Returning to the rest of the family, two other girls, Mary and Claire, and a boy, John, ranging from nine to seventeen, he asked if they knew anything about the trip. They knew nothing and a typical family domestic scene developed with the youngest saying it "wasn't fair" that they couldn't go anywhere in the car on such a lovely day and they didn't know where the others had gone. Sydney sensibly pointed out that it was after all their mother's birthday and perhaps they should be thinking of something to do to welcome her home when she did return.

Meanwhile Gladys and Ann had collected Peggy Pollard at her home and driven to Liskeard. Peggy kept them both amused on the journey with her quick wit and dry sense of humour, often interspersed as usual with quotations from the Bible and elsewhere. At last after driving round Liskeard in circles (it happens to everyone who does not know the exact whereabouts of Ladye Park), they arrived at the top of the Mass Path. The next half hour was an experience, which stayed vividly with both of them for the rest of their lives, for Ann another 32 and Gladys 40 years.

Above: The Mass path

Below: The house, nestling amongst trees

Chaptra Tri

(Chapter Three)
Park an Arloehes godrigys arta
Ladye Park revisited

Gladys, Ann and Peggy stood high up on Old Road Liskeard, and looked over the valley stretching before them. Nestling in among the trees, at the foot of the valley, was an 18th century farmhouse behind which rose a beautiful greenwood. No other habitation could be seen. On both sides of the farmhouse were fields bounded by high Cornish hedges. It was a site which all three of them realised had probably been the same for hundreds, even thousands of years, although the farmhouse had obviously changed. The scenery too would, of course, have changed with the seasons. Now it was a sight to behold with the new greens of Spring contrasting with the dark green of the greenwood and various shades in between. A myriad of primroses adorned the hedgerows.

"That's Ladye Park," announced Peggy in a matter of fact voice, showing just a hint of excitement, and at that same moment both Gladys and Ann felt they were stepping back in time. A few steps further down the road they turned into what appeared to be a track leading to a farm gate, but then Peggy turned abruptly left and they found themselves standing at the top of the most delightful footpath imaginable. High hedges bordered the narrow uneven path which meandered downwards. In places the tree branches hung over forming an arch making the way quite dark, but wherever there was a clearing large enough for the sun to penetrate an abundance of wild flowers was to be seen.

"This must be the Mass Path you've talked so much about," exclaimed Gladys in awe.

"Yes" replied Peggy with enthusiasm, "and just think of the countless pilgrims in the past who have walked this way; royalty with their entourage, and gentry, for there was once a royal hunting lodge situated in Ladye Park There would also, of course, have been hundreds upon hundreds of ordinary folk making their way to the chapel at the bottom for Mass or coming to the end of their long pilgrimage, having walked miles to get here. One day I'm going to write a book and call it 'Ladye Park Tales' and it will be a skit on the Canterbury Tales. Cornwall won't know what has hit it when the rest of the world reads them, but I'll make sure mine are proper pilgrims. After all who'd have gone on a pilgrimage all those years ago unless they really believed they were out to save their soul. They'd be crazy if they didn't. After all they weren't the cushy package trips we go on nowadays. Nevertheless I'd make sure they had lots of fun because I want to prove to the whole world that God is FUN. Anyway lets start the rosary now. I always say the joyful mysteries as I go down. I particularly like the second mystery, the visitation, because I feel I am en route with Mary, carrying Jesus in her womb, as she visits Elizabeth. Would you like to start Ann?"

And so they descended the path, probably more than two thousand years old, joyfully praying the rosary, communing with nature and aligning themselves with all pilgrims past and future who had travelled, and hopefully would travel that route to give glory to their God.

Suddenly the path opened out, and an abundance of stinging nettles, which had encroached upon the path momentarily barred their way. "Good penance for a pilgrim's sins," proclaimed Peggy with a laugh in her voice, as she strode straight through in spite of the open leather sandals she wore, winter and summer alike, on her stockingless feet. Gladys and Ann were not quite so sure that such penance was the order of the day, but a very convenient stick lay on the ground nearby. They recognised this as an excellent implement for beating down the undergrowth and so passed safely through, finding themselves on the lane bordering the grounds of Ladye Park. Exactly opposite was the tiny wooden gate, first seen by Peggy in the previous November.

The three did not have permission to enter the grounds or an appointment with the farmer, but Peggy eloquently described her previous visit and pointed out the stream and baptistery which could be seen from the road. Gladys and Ann said afterwards, that not being able to enter made no difference, they both had an indescribable feeling that they were indeed at a holy place.

"I think we should say at least one of the sorrowful mysteries here, just because it's so sad that it has been forgotten for so long. Let's just say the first, the "The Agony in the Garden" but I think we should concentrate on the word 'mystery' because I feel there's a mystery about this place too." said Peggy in her usual way of making the reciting of the rosary the most natural thing in the world. And so the three of them allying themselves with pilgrims of bygone years recited the rosary.

After spending a further 10 - 15 minutes wandering along the lane bordering the property and drinking in the atmosphere, they returned up the Mass Path and back to the car. The return journey to Truro took about 90 minutes. As on the outward journey Peggy was the ideal companion, regaling them with humorous ditties and stories. At one point she recited what she called a nursery rhyme for silly souls.

"For God
Look abroad-
He'll be found
All around,
He opens his treasure
To give you pleasure,
When you're hurt and you yell,
He'll kiss the place well,
And experience will show
That he never lets go.

For Sin
Look within-
The foul part of IRE
Boils on your fire.
the soup of SELF-PITY
Is greasy and gritty,
RESENTMENT's the fume,

That fills the whole room,
IMPATIENCE the mouse
That infests the whole house.

Call on MARY
In any quandary-
The mother of Grace,
Will plead your case,
Get you out of a hole,
Advise and console-
And then she devises
Such lovely surprises!

   After dropping Peggy off at her home, Gladys and Ann pulled in to their own house courtyard. Sydney greeted them and they soon began to explain the reason for their disappearance for the day.

   Although pleased that they had had an enjoyable day and that the car was back in one piece, he could not share their excitement and took the story of Peggy's 'vision' very much with a pinch of salt, not giving it a second thought.

   Over the next week Ladye Park or Peggy Pollard were possibly mentioned occasionally, but as in any family, most of the time was spent on normal everyday activities, cooking, washing, working, shopping and children's homework, so when Gladys's husband, Sydney, went in to Barclays Bank Trustee Dept, where he was manager, on 25th April, ten days after the memorable visit, his thoughts were not about anything in particular, and certainly not concerned with where his wife had been on her birthday.

   Mr Riche always liked to get into the office early to go through the post before the rest of the staff arrived. He could usually tell from the envelopes which ones could be dealt with by his secretary or other members of staff. The first letter he opened was in an innocuous handwritten brown envelope. He slit it open, saw it was merely an income tax query, and was about to put it on the pile for someone else to deal with when the address caught his eye. LADYE PARK LISKEARD. The name rang a bell. When had he heard that name before? Then it dawned on him! Of course! That was where his wife said she had been on her birthday. He felt it somewhat a coincidence that the name should be brought to his attention, so instead of immediately passing the letter on, he went to the filing cabinet to investigate further. He found that Ladye Park was the subject of a trust with which his department was dealing, and what is more the very deeds were in his safe! He began to read further.

He discovered that a 99 year lease had been made on the property from 24th June 1865 with a rent of £5 per annum payable on 24th June each year. The agents at the time had been Haye & Scad Morgan of Liskeard. The income from the estate was to be paid to two children Edward Vincent Carthew and Eileen Constance and then to their children. The value of the property in 1865 had been £1,200. Looking further into the file he realised that, with only nine years left on a 99 year lease, the bank as trustees should start planning in conjunction with the legatees as to what should happen to the property when the lease expired. At this point Mr Riche was merely pleased that he had been alerted to a job which needed attention.

Although a man of strong religious faith, having been converted to Catholicism some years previously, Sydney Riche's beliefs tended to be a private matter. He was excellent at his job, very ethical and moral, but these qualities were not a result of his religious convictions. He would have been the first to admit that his colleagues of more secular dispositions shared those same qualities. He had chosen his religion (having spent many years searching before finally finding the Catholic Church), because it upheld the beliefs he already possessed and seemed right for him. He did not hide his Catholicism, particularly at the yearly Bank Dinner Dance, which was always held on a Friday (a day of abstinence from meat in those pre-Vatican II days). He would phone the hotel beforehand to order a special fish dish for Gladys and himself. He was always the envy of his astounded fellow diners, when waiters appeared, carrying two individually prepared gourmet fish dishes. When asked why he had such preferential treatment, he had no hesitation in explaining that Catholics refrained from eating meat on Fridays as a form of penance. As far as he was concerned penance did not come into it, but at least he felt he was being a witness and left the situation at that.

Like most Catholics, at the time, Sydney did not believe in individuals getting communication direct from God, but through the Church. He would have been the first to say that there would be chaos if everyone started believing that they were being told directly by God what they should or should not do. As for believing in signs and wonders that was a non-starter for him. Yes, he believed in the Bible, but that happened long ago. In 1956 one was expected to believe in those events of the past, say one's prayers, live one's life the way Christ would want - and Sydney accepted the Church's teaching on this. The idea of God still choosing individuals to perform certain tasks was foreign to him. However, by the end of that 25th April 1956 he was convinced that noticing the name 'Ladye Park' on the letter had not been a coincidence. It had not been brought to his attention just because an expiry date on a trust had been overlooked. He firmly believed in the light of the strange story his wife had told him that somehow he too was being drawn into something he could not quite fathom. He was a man very used to being in full command of every situation. This feeling was new to him. He decided to call on Mrs Pollard after work. He, like many others in the town had always known Peggy simply as "Mrs Pollard", which seemed a little less formal than 'Dr' but neither of them would have dreamt of calling the other by their Christian name. Her flat was almost directly opposite his office in Pydar Street, Truro.

91, Stret Pydar
91, Pydar Street

Mrs Pollard's abode was not a salubrious one. To reach her two roomed second floor flat Mr Riche had to enter a double fronted gardenless house and climb some dark uncarpeted wooden stairs. At the top was the bathroom, which looked as though it might be shared with another flat. He turned to the left along a narrow corridor as he had been instructed on the phone earlier. The door of the first room was slightly ajar, and inside he could just see an enormous desk covered with papers and books and still more were piled or just scattered all over the floor. That, he had been forewarned, was 'Pollard's room'. Pollard, her husband, known to many as "The Captain" was a familiar character in the town. He had been the commander of a mine sweeper during the war. He was over six feet tall, weighed 26 stone and had a large bushy beard. He was on Cornwall County Council and countless other committees and obviously had to deal with a great deal of paper work. The adjacent room was Mrs Pollard's own room and this door was open too, as he had been told it would be.

Still in his dark business suit and carrying his briefcase, Sydney knocked and entered. It was a large airy room. The left hand wall was covered with black silhouette heads of Dr Pollard's friends. Instead of the modern day practice of asking visitors to sign a visitor's book, Dr Pollard asked them to stand under a light, whilst she drew around their shadow and then painted it in. In the right hand corner was a large grand piano, stacked high with music, a guitar lay on the floor, and there were a couple of music stands, one of which held a hand written score. Above the piano was a wall covered in framed paintings and on either side of the bay window, directly opposite the door, were two life-sized paintings of monks. One was St Dominic, her favourite saint, and the other Blessed Martin de Porres (now St. Martin de Porres). In the bay itself was a very old chaise-longue. It was obviously antique, but in dire need of restoration. Draped over it was a beautiful tapestry cover. In fact all the chairs looked as though they were in need of repair and Sydney momentarily wondered if any were safe to sit on. All were upholstered with the most exquisite tapestry work, for Dr Pollard was an expert needle woman. The table was good solid oak, covered by an embroidered tablecloth. On the floor was a large, loose, hand-woven carpet, very old and worn, surrounded by bare floorboards. Although at the beginning of the twenty first century stripped floor boards and loose carpets are fashionable once more, this floor bore no resemblance to its modern day counterpart. The floorboards had not even been stained, just plain rough wood.

Along the fourth wall there were bookcases, almost ceiling-high and full of leather-bound books, a gasfire and one small gas ring on which Peggy cooked everything hot which she and Pollard ate.

Peggy rose to meet Mr Riche as he entered the room. She had been a beauty in her youth and this still showed. She wore no make-up but her eyes, a clear blue, were both piercing and kindly at the same time. She was tall and slim. Her waist-length dark hair hung loosely in a net. Around her head she wore a scarf, tied peasant fashion, and over her long flowing black skirt a beige hessian apron. Both were heavily embroidered. She looked to all intents and purposes like a Russian peasant, except that around her waist was a thick black leather belt from which hung her rosary beads. Mr Riche was not surprised by her appearance, for he had seen her countless times striding around the town, always dressed the same except that in Winter she wore a black jumper and in Summer a black blouse. Her legs were always stockingless and she never wore a coat.

Now she moved towards him with grace and elegance. Grasping his hand warmly to welcome him, she said in her beautiful cultured voice with just a hint of a Cornish accent: "How nice of you to call Mr Riche, but I know this is not just a social call, you are far too busy for that, so tell me, to what do I owe this honour? "

Mr Riche did not beat about the bush. He explained that he had been told her story by his wife, that at first it had just been a story and nothing else, but that that day's events had made him think that he could perhaps be of help to her. He asked her how she envisaged carrying out Our Lady's wishes, to which she replied: "Well presumably Our Lady will arrange it all. I don't intend doing anything drastic unless I get the definite proof that I asked for. Although I have heard nothing yet about my picture, I feel from all the things which have been happening, Our Lady has already been giving me proof, and I have a wonderful feeling of excitement about the whole thing. I suppose my part will be to purchase the old shrine and then to hand it over to the bishop. After that it will be up to him."

Mrs. Pollard was at the time a wealthy woman and although completely unmaterialistic for herself, as witness her lifestyle, she would have been in a position to purchase the shrine and Mr Riche was aware of this. He explained to her his position as regards the bank, that his loyalty must at all times be to it, and the bank's clients but he thought that his involvement could be mutually beneficial if, as was very likely, the trust beneficiaries who were not in the country, decided they wished to sell. The two parted company with Mr Riche promising to follow the matter up and with Mrs Pollard saying she would be most grateful for any information as to how she could purchase the shrine site.

To Peggy this visit from Mr Riche was yet another sign that Our Lady really did mean business. When she heard the following day that "La Vierge à la Porcelaine" had been selected for hanging in the Paris salon Summer Exhibition, her joy knew no bounds. She wrote to the Bishop of Plymouth, informing him of the latest development and telling him to expect a purchase in the near future!

On the 30th April 1956 Mrs Pollard received a personal reply from the bishop.

Vescourt
Hartley
Plymouth
Telephone Crownhill 77179
28th April 1956

Dear Mrs. Pollard,

I am very pleased indeed to receive your letter this morning and to hear your encouraging news, and I shall look forward to having more details from Father Hackett as soon as the matter has been arranged. In the meantime I thank you sincerely for your help and pray that Our Blessed Lady will guide us all in the re-establishment of her Shrine.

Yours devotedly in Christ,
Cyril
Bishop of Plymouth

Stream flowing into baptistry at Ladye Park

Chaptra Peswar

(Chapter Four)
Kesanj lytherow
Exchange of Letters

The following morning Mr Riche returned to the Ladye Park file. He wanted to study the deeds to see whether there was any separate mention of the shrine site, as the whole estate consisted of a farm, farmhouse with out buildings, and some woodland. There was a separate plan for the shrine site, but then what interested him even more was that he discovered half of the property was leasehold on a lease of 99 years from 24.6.1865 and the other half was freehold, but there was nothing to show the exact extent of the leasehold. In fact it looked as if the dividing line went directly through the farmhouse. He realised this was something which would need to be sorted out, so he wrote to Mr Kelly, the first of many letters to various correspondents, with reference to Ladye Park:

30th April 1956
To:
H Kelly Esq
Ladye Park
Liskeard

Dear Sir,
<u>Edward James Carthew Settlement</u>

As you know, we are the Trustees of the Edward James Carthew Settlement, one of the assets being the leasehold portion of Ladye Park. The lease expires on 24th June 1964 and it seems that when that date arrives there is likely to be some difficulty because the dividing line of the leasehold and freehold property passes through the dwelling house.

I have never seen the property as the collection of the ground rent has been left to our Agents. I shall be in Liskeard next Saturday afternoon, May 5th, and would like to take the opportunity of calling on you about 6.30 p.m. when you or your son could show me the property and, in particular, *where you consider the dividing line between the leasehold and freehold, runs.*

Unless I hear from you to the contrary, I shall assume the day and time are convenient

Yours faithfully

S. W. Riche (Manager)

No reply arrived, so on Saturday 5th May 1956 Mr Riche drove to Liskeard, parked his car outside Ladye Park for the first time, entered via the small wooden gate and knocked on the farmhouse door. He was welcomed by both Mr Kelly and his son and led through the house to a large kitchen dominated by the traditional Cornish range with a kettle boiling on the hob. Discussion about the extent of the leasehold began almost immediately and Mr Kelly said that there was no problem whatsoever about where the dividing line went. He knew exactly where it was and he assured Mr Riche that he only lived in his half. The other half had been empty for as long as he could remember. Surprised at this, Mr Riche asked if he could be shown around, and sure enough half of the rooms were absolutely empty of furniture and the sitting room had a dresser, sideboard, small table, and armchairs, all in one half of the room and the other half was completely bare including the walls.

"You see," explained the farmer "the line goes straight through the middle of this room, and we never use that side."

Mr Riche could not believe what he was hearing or seeing.

"I'm amazed," he said, "that you stick so rigidly to your tenancy agreement. Surely you didn't think it would matter if you used the rooms while you were the only people here?"

"Oh no," came the quick response, "as long as we stick to our part, the bees don't bother us but as soon as we go over the line we get stung. They've got their rooms and we've got ours and we're happy to keep it like that."

"Bees?" queried Mr Riche "What do you mean?"

It turned out that bees had been living at Ladye Park as long as anyone could remember. They were rather a vicious swarm and on several occasions pest controllers had been brought in to get rid of them, but to no avail. They had taken up residence in the roof and in one room the honey actually dripped through the ceiling. Kelly said all the locals knew about them and rumour had it that anyone who did manage to get rid of them would suffer bad luck. He didn't believe in all that rubbish, but he had found that whenever he and his family ventured into the bees' side of the house, they were stung and that was pretty bad luck if anything was. As the bees' side coincided with the opposite side to his, he decided it would be best to let them keep it. Since then, he explained, none of his family had ever been stung.

This was one of the strangest stories Mr Riche had come across in his visits for the Bank. He was not very knowledgeable about bees, but none seemed to be flying around while he was there, for which he was very grateful, as he did not fancy getting stung.

Mr Riche then moved on to the subject of the shrine and asked Kelly whether he was aware that there had once been a place of Christian devotion on the spot. He replied that he had vaguely heard something about there having been a chapel, or some such place there. He had also heard that it once belonged to royalty, but he did not know much about it. Mr Riche then told him that there was a lady, who was interested in restoring a medieval shrine, which had stood there and asked whether he would have any objections. Kelly's response was that he had been thinking of buying the reversion and if that happened he would be quite happy to sell off the shrine site. Mr Riche offered to discuss sale of the reversion to Kelly, but said he would need to arrange for a valuer to call. Kelly seemed content with this arrangement and Mr Riche left, calling on Fr Hackett on the way home to inform him of the situation.

A local valuer was contacted, but when after a couple of weeks,

Mr Riche had heard nothing, he wrote to Fr Hackett suggesting that he call at Ladye Park to try to establish whether the valuer had called.

Fr Hackett replied in a handwritten letter:

The Presbytery
West Hill
Liskeard

June 6th 1956

Dear Mr Riche,

Many thanks for your letter but I am afraid I have nothing to report. It seems to me we will need great patience with the Kellys. The old man said he had a very unsatisfactory answer from the valuer. He wanted Kelly to reveal the value already put on the place, so Kelly didn't even answer the letter and says now he will have nothing more to do with the sale. It seems the son is in charge from now on and when I've called I haven't been able to see the son. However I'll call again and see if I can't get something definite.

It seems to me the Kellys are not in any hurry and the only hope is to keep on asking and urging them to act. It is all very disappointing and at present I don't see what can be done except hope and pray that the delay will not be long.

Yours very sincerely,
Fr Hackett

Several more letters went to and fro and eventually a value of £675 was put on the leasehold, but Kelly turned this down saying he was not interested after all. This put Dr Pollard in a quandary. She had already been taken over to meet the farmer by Mr Riche. She desperately wanted to get on and fulfil the commission she believed she had been given, but if Kelly was happy as he was, everything seemed to be stalemate. She therefore decided that a way out would be for her to purchase the land herself, so she wrote a letter to Mr Kelly.

THE LOST SHRINE OF LISKEARD

91, Pydar Street
Truro
6th July 1956

Dear Mr Kelly,

About a month ago I came over with Mr Riche, and we met your son. Mr Riche mentioned to him that I was very interested in preserving the site of the old shrine.

Now I wonder whether you would be agreeable to my making an offer for the reversion of the leasehold. I am very anxious that everything should be with your good will. You might perhaps find it convenient to let me buy the leasehold, on condition that you yourself had all the rights of way and access as you wished, and the use of the whole dwelling house (which I understand forms part of the leasehold,) and that as your landlord I should not ask you for any rent at all during the rest of your lease. The part we are really interested in is the orchard where the baptistery stands, with the stream, and also the well - but of course there would be no question of interfering with your present use of the well. In fact it would be the same from your point of view as if you yourself had bought the reversion and sold me the strip of land that you first said you would be willing to sell.

I would do everything I could to meet your convenience, and it is likely that at the end of your lease, if you wished to sell the whole farm, we would be able to make you an acceptable offer. In the meantime such an arrangement would mean that you would not have to spend a penny but would actually gain whatever it is that the leasehold at present costs you in rent.

I wish to be fair and honest about this and am telling you about it before I make an offer to the Trustees; for should you be anxious to buy the reversion yourself at the agent's valuation, I hope to make you an offer for the piece of land we have discussed.

Yours,
Margaret S. Pollard

Having received no reply a month later, Mrs Pollard felt she could wait no longer, so wrote directly to the agents dealing with Ladye Park.

91, Pydar St
Truro
Vosper & Kivell Estate Agents
2, Greenbank Rd
Liskeard
July 9th 1956

Dear Sirs,

<u>Ladye Park</u>

I am interested in the preservation of the old shrine of Our Lady in the Park, which I understand to be part of the farm called Ladye Park, and to be leasehold.

Before the war when I was Hon. Secretary of the Cornwall Branch of the C.P.R.E., I was instrumental in preserving two holy wells, and am now anxious similarly to see preserved this very interesting site, which contains a well and a small building, supposed to be a baptistery.

Barclays Bank Trustee Dept., to whom I applied, refer me to you for a price. I do not know how large the area is but assume the well is included. I understand that the farmer uses it as a water supply, and naturally his use of it would not be interfered with. But I should be glad to know if it is included in the site.

Some time ago I had a chat with Kelly about preserving the site of the shrine. Had he intended to purchase the leasehold himself I hoped to come to some arrangement with him. But I understand now that he is not interested in making an offer; so I should like to do so myself.

Will you please let me know what price is wanted for the reversion of the leasehold?

Yours faithfully

(Mrs Pollard)

The response to this letter was most promising. The agent contacted Mr Kelly who changed his mind again, and said he would buy the reversion and sell the shrine site to Mrs Pollard for £200. She was delighted and immediately informed Mr Riche who said the Bishop of Plymouth should be informed and the following letter was duly written.

Trenerry House,
Bodmin Road,
Truro
Phone 2849

16th July 1956

The Right Rev. Cyril Restieaux
Bishop of Plymouth,
Vescourt,
Hartley,
Plymouth.

My Lord Bishop,

Ladye Park, Liskeard

As you know, Mrs Pollard of Truro has taken steps during the last few months to restore the shrine at Liskeard. I understand she is writing to you separately giving you the latest position and has suggested that I should write also, informing you of the present position from the "business" angle.

I am the Manager of Barclays Bank Ltd., Trustee Department, Truro, and one of the properties under my control is the freehold of Ladye Park, the lease of which is owned by Mr H. Kelly. This lease has eight years to run. Mr Kelly has now agreed to buy the freehold reversion from the Trustees, and he in turn has agreed to sell to Mrs Pollard, for £200, that part of the land on which the shrine stood.

This was agreed verbally with Mr Kelly on Friday evening last, after which we saw Fr Hackett of Liskeard. He thought that, as Mrs Pollard intended to make a gift of the land to Plymouth Diocese, it would be preferable if the contract was signed by him, on behalf of the Church. I understand that Fr Hackett will be communicating with one of your secretaries concerning this.

Mrs Pollard has already handed over the various sums to Fr Hackett totalling in all, I believe, £641.13s 0d to be used for the restoration of the shrine. As further money may be coming in from time to time I have suggested to Fr Hackett that the shrine money is kept separate from Parish money.

I am of course extremely interested in the proposed restoration and feel very privileged to have been associated with its early stages. For the moment the matter rests with Fr Hackett and his advisers to see that a contract is signed. I have given my word to Mr Kelly that the contract, for the sale of the land to the Church, will be signed at the same time as he is asked to sign the contract for the purchase of the reversion, so that he will know that he need not find the purchase price.

Under normal conditions the land is not worth £200, but Mrs Pollard is prepared to pay almost anything to get the shrine into Catholic hands again and as she is providing the money I do not think any query will be raised on this. In a matter of this nature it is essential to keep the goodwill of Mr Kelly and I think this has been done.

I am at your disposal, to render any further assistance I can.

I have the Honour to be

Your Lordship's Devoted and Obedient Child

S.W. Riche

Skolheyk Maria, Martin Gillett, a omgyv kevrennek y'n dra
Mariologist Martin Gillett becomes involved

Most organisations slow down over the Summer months due to personnel holiday leave and this was the case with the bishop's office. Mr Riche received a letter of acknowledgement with an explanation that the letter would be dealt with in late August when the bishop and his secretary would both be back in Plymouth. This was completely understandable, but Dr Pollard was fired with enthusiasm and already had visions of Liskeard becoming a great place of pilgrimage once more. She equated it with Lourdes, Fatima and Walsingham and all the other holy places she had visited.

All these places of Marian devotion had their own statues. She felt sure that if Our Lady of the Park had been a well known shrine it must have had its own statue. The one person she knew, who would know about this, was Martin Gillett, a well known Anglican mariologist, who had recently produced the map of English shrines, marking "Our Lady of the Park - no longer in existence." She therefore wrote to him to ask for any information he had. He admitted he knew nothing about a statue and very little at all about the history, but he would love it, if a visit could be arranged for him, and so the following week Martin Gillett arrived by train at Liskeard railway station and Mrs Pollard was there to meet him. The arrangement was that he would then stay for a few days with Mr Riche, who had arranged for him to visit St. Michaels Mount. She escorted him to Ladye Park. He was delighted with what he saw, but he felt the real focal point was the pool and niche - that he felt was the real Holy Well and not the "house well" at all. He became very excited and said he would write an article about it for the 'Catholic Herald'. He would have to liaise with Fr Hackett and he also said he felt he should approach the bishop himself, because without his explicit approval it would not be expedient to give any publicity to it.

After Martin Gillett's return Mrs Pollard had slight reservations about articles being written and approaches being made to the bishop before anything had been finalised, so she wrote to Mr

Gillett again, asking him to "hang fire" for a while. In reply Mr Gillett wrote:

...Except that I have communicated with the Bishop, in confidence, you may be sure that I know when to keep things sub rosa As whatever work I do is by the nature of it, to be authoritative, it is my rule to involve myself in nothing which anticipates promotion of cultus without at least the tacit approval of the bishop in each case.

As a matter of fact, I had Our Lady of the Park on my list for a good many years, since 1939 in fact, as one of the key shrines which ought to be aroused as soon as possible. Our Lady of the Taper got in first simply because, as soon as the map appeared in 1953, the Bishop of Menevia wrote to me himself and laid the way open for all that has in fact happened. But as you know I ventured to put 'The Park' on the map. Then in May in my last article on the subject in the 'Catholic Herald', I concluded with the express hope that four others which I named might now begin to move: Liskeard, Jesmond, Ipswich and Worcester so you will see there is no question of leakage. I do not regard it as 'coincidence' that you have been moved to act in Cornwall, but as a direct sign that Our Lady may wish it. Curiously, within a fortnight of the article there was a pilgrimage to Our Lady's old shrine at Jesmond. I am in touch with people who are moving things there.

In the meantime I will write again in a day or two, when I have really had time to check the papers you have so kindly entrusted me with; and will go on praying that all the rough places may be made smooth. Then we can go into details for a statue. The fleur-de-lys must be preserved. I had already a note of it.

My approach to the Bishop was purely formal - not to involve `  . ` in any way beyond his assent that I should be interested in certain aspects. His reply was quite reassuring.

Martin Gillett.

Mr Riche also received a letter sometime later. It was the customary 'thank you letter', which began with general pleasantries but *continued* with some very interesting historical information.

86, West Hill
Putney, London S.W.15

Dear Mr Riche,

... I made a snap decision to try and run through some of the <u>Patent</u> *and <u>Close</u> Rolls of Edward II, III and Richard II as regards Ladye Park. I found perhaps more than I hoped for. The evidence is clear that Liskeard was a Royal Park, at least in the time of Edward II (I have not touched earlier, yet) and that in 1316 the grant was made, during the King's pleasure, to Roger de Aqua, King's Chaplain of the chapel of St Mary in the King's Park of Liskeard. It fits into the pattern of history that by 1318, the rights of the Park had been made over to Queen Isabella; and by 1332 this was held by the King's brother, John, Earl of Cornwall. On his death, he was succeeded by Edward, Duke of Cornwall. From this it seems clear that the Park was regarded as an integral part of the estates pertaining to the Earls, later dukes, of Cornwall. It will be necessary to go back earlier now, and see what was there before the earldom was absorbed by the Crown.*

There were not always hermits there, as some good books say, but the Chapel of Our Lady of the Park was normally served, as a Chapel Royal, by king's Chaplains; thus being independent of episcopal visitation. But at least one hermit there was. His name was Roger Goodman, and he appears after the death of John, Earl of Cornwall, temp. Edward III. Later, 1379, Richard II confirms (? reverts to the older custom) the appointment of Richard Legge, King's Chaplain, to say Mass in the <u>King's Chapel within the Old Park</u> of Liskeard.

In one swoop to have found so much is valuable. Sometimes one can go for days and find nothing at all...next time I will try to tackle earlier documents, and also the Chantry Inquisitions. I suppose even though a chapel Royal, Saint-Mary's-in-the-Park ranked as a Chantry....and it may even be possible to find some chantry endowment somewhere. I think this likely, and that the hermit was supplementary to a Chaplain because the latter had to have a Protection (with the clause Rogamus) to collect alms for his subsistence, which a chaplain of a chapel Royal would not have required.

Through the erections of various commissions of Oyer & Terminer (because of trespass upon the king's park there) one is able to keep fairly good check upon the actual holder of park rights...almost invariably the king's son who became Earl (or duke) of Cornwall, but twice, either a widow, or the King's widow, she deriving Dowry therefrom .... I think I am right in saying that it is rare that a holy well *by itself was ever the sole focus of a pilgrimage to Our Lady. There was always a chapel too. The Mass was considered an integral part of the pilgrimage .....*

Yours very sincerely
H. Martin Gillett

Having been informed that no statue of Our Lady of the Park seemed to be in existence, Dr Pollard decided to have some fun and try and make one herself. She had recently been attending pottery classes. She was still very much a novice and needed projects to work on at the classes. When she told her instructor that she intended making a statue, she was advised against it, being told that she had not yet learnt the skills necessary. However, undeterred she made up her mind to have a go. She made a small clay statue, modelled on the painting, which was hung in the Paris Salon. Her teacher was still not impressed.

"You are using clay, not plasticine," he pointed out. "You can just let it dry out and keep it for a while but there is no point in firing it. It will just crack and fall to bits."

"If it breaks it breaks" was Mrs Pollard's reply, "I'd like to give it a go. Nothing ventured, nothing gained."

Reluctantly he agreed saying that he would only allow the firing to go ahead, because it was summer time and so most students were on holiday. Consequently there was room in the kiln and she could learn from her mistakes. That was fine by Mrs Pollard. The whole project was only for a "bit of fun" anyway.

The following week she was greeted by Mr Lane the potter with:
"Well, I've got to eat humble pie. I think it's a miracle but your statue has fired!"

The glazing stage went off equally well and by the 20th August 1956 it was gracing her flat in Pydar Street. Mr Lane's idea of a miracle was not quite the same as Dr Pollard's, but she did feel that there must have been a little divine intervention in saving it from destruction, so with her belief that miracles (even minor ones) are always performed for a purpose, she thought that what she was meant to do was to place the statue somewhere at Ladye Park. On 27th August therefore, she went to Liskeard once more, this time with two friends named David Clarke and Mary Furze and they took the statue with them. There was no-one around so they were able to wander undisturbed. They decided to put it in a niche, behind a lintel, over the stream where it fitted perfectly and was invisible, if one did not know it was there.

The weather was not good, the bushes overhanging the water made the area very dark, but David Clarke took a photo of the statue in its new home, using a time exposure. To their later surprise the photo came out very well and when it was sent to Fr Esmond in Malta, he felt there was an "uncanny" resemblance to Mrs Pollard's original water colour. Any visitor to the spot (even today when the whole structure has undergone a restoration programme) would be amazed at the similarity in shape and form of the cave like formation in the stream by the baptistery with the cave in the painting, "La Vierge à la Porcelaine" and yet it was painted before Dr Pollard had ever been to Ladye Park and before she knew of the existence of water there.

Above: The legendary King Caradoc of Cornwall,
as depicted on a modern mural by David Whittley

Below: King Doniert's Stone

Chaptra Pymp
(Chapter Five)
Kan an mor y'n eglos
A Sea Shanty in Church

Having successfully completed her statue project, and still with the vision of future pilgrimages to Ladye Park on the lines of other Marian shrines, Dr Pollard set about writing a Ladye Park hymn. She was an accomplished musician able to transpose any tune at sight and had composed many pieces in her time, both secular and religious. To her, music was for enjoyment, and she enjoyed all types. She was just as much at home playing French nursery ballads to children on her guitar as she was playing a piano concerto, although she always said her favourite music was the dance music of her youth. It seems that at the age of seventeen she loved dancing and her favourite partner was her brother, who had been an expert dancer.

The congregation at church became used to her playing hymns to secular tunes. She was a great believer in the adage, "Why should the devil have all the good music?" She acted as organist at every church service. In one of the letters she wrote to Gladys from the Isolation Hospital when she had measles she wrote,

"I'm not altogether sorry to have a water-tight alibi for the stations of the cross which frankly I find a bit of a chore - one day I shall play that hymn (*English version of Stabat Mater ed*) to "MEN OF HARLECH"

On another occasion she was asked to play the organ for the funeral of a seafarer. Her husband, Pollard, had warned her that he doubted whether any of the mourners had darkened a church for a long time and certainly not a Catholic one, so Fr Wharton the parish priest thought his ears were playing him up when he heard "A life on the ocean waves" being played as the coffin was borne into the church. The music for the rest of the service was of the same ilk, ending up with 'Over the Blue horizon' and afterwards she was surrounded by mourners, saying they had no idea funerals could be such fun and how much the Captain would have enjoyed it.

"Would have!" she retorted, "I hope he DID. I'm presuming all the angels and saints in heaven, not to mention his old pals, were joining in singing to welcome him through the pearly gates to meet his maker"

Her main aim, as far as hymns were concerned, was to ensure the congregation sang. As she always said, "No-on can join in the words unless they know the tune." Her thought therefore in writing a Ladye Park pilgrimage hymn was to have a tune which was catchy, and which everyone would be able to join in. The Lourdes "Ave Maria" was recognised everywhere as a hymn to Our Lady and was very easy to sing whilst walking in procession. She felt she needed something like that. Although she was more than capable of composing a completely new tune she felt strongly that as Ladye Park had such history the hymn should be set to a traditional tune. She chose 'Daily, daily, sing to Mary' and the words she wrote were:

1. **Lady Mary, Blessed Mother,**
Whom we hail as full of grace,
Whom our Cornish fathers honoured
In this green and peaceful place,
Pilgrims from the stony moorlands
Through the rain and wind and dark,
Loving Mary, praising Mary,
Lady Mary of the Park.

2. **Poor men tramping, rich men riding,**
All Our Lady came to greet;
Wife and widow, youth and maiden
Gathered at the Virgin's feet.
Of God's justice she is mirror,
Of his covenant the ark,
Blessed Mary, Holy Mary,
Lady Mary of the Park.

3. Grazing deer deep in the forest
Heard the pilgrims' joyful song,
And the birds among the branches
Sang in chorus with the throng;
Wren and robin, thrush and blackbird
And the heavenward-soaring lark
Sang to Mary, Blessed Mary,
Lady Mary of the Park

4. Then came evil men to plunder
And destroyed the forest shrine.
Dark was now the lamp of Mary-
Yet there still was left a sign.
For the pure clear well of water
Held its secret in the dark,
Longed for Mary, dreamed of Mary,
Lady Mary of the Park

5.Now returning, we will praise thee,
For the peril is long past.
Come again O blessed Mother,
And reclaim thy shrine at last.
To the promised land in safety
God has brought his sacred ark,
And we praise thee, Blessed Mary
Lady Mary of the Park

It could well be assumed that with her love of the secular combined with the spiritual, Dr Pollard would have welcomed the new simpler hymns, which began to appear after Vatican II, but far from it, she abhorred them. To her mind they did nothing to enhance the beauty of the Mass and other liturgical services. She regarded them as entirely without artistic, cultural, or spiritual merit. Nor did they present a 'holy fun element.' She accepted that one man's meat is another man's poison, but to her a solemn high Mass transported one on to a spiritual plane, giving a glimpse of the glory of heaven even more than did her daily low Mass, where she was able to concentrate on the wonderful words of scripture in addition to her meeting with the Lord in Holy Communion. She loved the Psalms, whether spoken or sung, and so when, more than 20 years after writing the first, she wrote a second hymn to Our Lady in the Park, she based it on the Scriptures she knew and loved. As she was a fluent Cornish speaker and a Cornish bard, she also gave it a Cornish chorus, the translation of which was:

Hail Mary, Hail Mary,
Heed us as we call to you,
Our loyalty affirming
Hail Mary full of Grace.

For this hymn she also composed the music

Processional hymn for Our Lady in the Park.

Come, O Queen, into your garden,
Lady like the moon in beauty,
Lady like the sun in glory,
Like an army bright with banners.
Stair by which the Lord descended,
Burning Bush revealed to Moses,
Land of Promise! Field of mercies!
Here your children's song of praise.
(Chorus) Hayl Marya! Hayl Marya!
Col orthyn warnas ow-crya,
Agan lelder owth-affya,
Hayl Marya lun a ras!

Come, O queen into your garden,
Bluebell-carpet spread beneath you,
Chestnut blossom arched above you,
Blackbird singing for your welcome;
Breathing out a richer perfume
Than the best of balm and balsam,

THE LOST SHRINE OF LISKEARD

Rose of Sharon! Fragrant lily!
Here your children's song of praise.
(**Chorus**)

Mother both of lamb and shepherd
Lead your faithful sheep to pasture
Lead the straying sheep to Jesus,
To the meadow of salvation;
To your Son O mother Mary
To the well of living water,
Sinners' Refuge! Help of Christians
Hear your children's song of praise.
(**Chorus**)

Of Fair Love she is the mother
Holy hope and fear and knowledge
She was chosen by the Father
To bestow his grace upon us
Morning star that brings the sunrise
Gate of Paradise is Mary;
Clement Virgin! Queen of Angels!
Hear your children's song of praise
(**Chorus**)

In the clearing of the forest
Shrine and spring to her were sacred
Thither came a host of pilgrims
As we come today to greet her
In the Royal Park of Mary
Safely feeds the flock of Jesus
Faithful Virgin! Wondrous Mother!
Hear your children's song of praise
(**Chorus**)
Set your foot upon the serpent
Sinless virgin, intercessor,
Wrap your veil about the lonely

Clasp the sinner to your bosom;
Tell your son the wine is failing
Tell us how To do his bidding
Queen of martyrs! Tower of David!
Hear your children's song of praise
(**Chorus**)

In your hand are sweet surprises,
Mercies not of our deserving;
She whose heart was pierced with sorrow
Best can read our secret longings.
Tried and tested was your patience,
You were blessed for your believing;
Mourners' comfort! Seat of Wisdom!
Hear your children's song of praise
(**Chorus**)

Fordh nowdyh a gentrynn hwithrans istorek
New road provokes historical research

So far, so good! Up until now everything seemed to be going to plan, and it looked as though Our Lady's shrine would be back up and running in no time, but this was not to be.

The bishop arrived back from his summer break to find a letter from Mr Riche, suggesting that the simplest way for the shrine site to be purchased would be for Mrs Pollard to buy it in her own name and then to hand it over to the Church. That way there would be no doubling up of solicitors letters or waiting for respective parties to return from holiday, etc.. The bishop replied on 1st September 1956 that, as far as the Church was concerned, that arrangement would be fine and they would now only come into the matter when Mrs Pollard was ready to make the site over to the diocese.

On the 14th September the first blow fell. Mr Riche received a letter from the Carthew family in New Zealand stating that they wanted nothing to do with the sale and that a letter giving fuller reasons would follow. Mrs Pollard was obviously very disappointed as was Fr Hackett, especially when November came and the promised 'letter following' had not arrived.

An urgent Income tax query caused Mr Riche to write to the Carthews again in December, but there was still no reply. Mrs Pollard became very impatient and when the New Year still produced nothing, she decided that the only way to get things moving was to ask Kelly, if she could rent the shrine site until such time as the sale could take place. She and Mr Riche made an appointment to visit him to discuss this proposal.

Mr Riche was also a local town councillor and at a meeting he attended the week prior to the appointment with Mr Kelly, he was presented with the agreed plans for the new A38, which was to run from Plymouth via Liskeard to Bodmin. A proposal had been made to build another new road linking Bodmin with Truro and that was to be the subject of the discussion, but as Mr Riche looked at the Liskeard part of the A38 plans, warning bells began to ring in his mind, for it looked as though it could be going straight through Ladye Park. He asked for a more detailed Ordinance Survey Map showing the exact location of the new road and his fears were confirmed, Ladye Park was to be demolished and the whole area destroyed so that the new road could be built.

On returning home he immediately rang Mrs Pollard to tell her the bad news but far from becoming despondent the news seemed to excite her.

"This must be the reason Our Lady appeared to me rather than anyone else. She knows I've had lots to do with preserving ancient wells and sites of interest. We'll just have to get the route changed."

"That's easier said than done" was his reply. "All plans have been passed and, as far as I know, a date has been set for the contractors to start work. At this late stage I don't see how anything can be done."

Undaunted she replied, "Surely with your influence you can do something."

"Would that I could, but if you'd like to do a little more research into the history of the shrine, so that we have something more than a hunch on your part, and a few letters from Martin Gillett, I will try and present a case, but don't raise your hopes too much as I personally feel our chances of success in this are very slim indeed."

And so all Dr Pollard's research skills were brought into play. Her fluent Cornish was an enormous help as she scoured all the Cornish literature, particularly the medieval miracle plays for mention of the shrine. She read old essays on Cornish history; she combed the libraries, she visited Liskeard and tirelessly sought out families who had been established in the area for generations, asking them whether they had any hearsay knowledge of the importance of the site or even any family legends.

Gradually a story began to unravel which was very much bigger than just a medieval shrine to Our Lady, dissolved at the Reformation. Unfortunately the notes giving exact references for the facts gathered are missing but the tale she narrated, countless times later, was that the story went back much much further to the days before Rome was built, when a belief in a goddess, known as Kerrid held sway in Cornwall. She was known as the goddess of love and eternal youth. In Wales she was known as Caridwen "The White Love (goddess)" hymned by Robert Graves in his famous book "The White Goddess" but in Cornwall she was known as Kerrid and her shrine was so important that a little Cornish town, Liskeard, which grew up nearby took its name from her.

. 'Lys' is Cornish for 'court.' In many old manuscripts Liskeard is spelt as 'Liskerd' and although the name is open to interpretation, it was Margaret Pollard's firm belief that it meant 'Court of Kerrid'. With the coming of Christianity it was customary for the traditional holy places to be christianised, holy wells were often given saints names, but Kerrid was too well loved and known. As locals were already accustomed to making pilgrimages to her 'Lys," her well was left, and a chapel built nearby so that the pilgrims could now focus on the Holy Mass for their pilgrimages with the hope that interest in the well would eventually diminish. And this of course was all on the same site, which Our Lady seemed to be asking Dr Pollard to set about re-opening. The chapel there was dedicated to the Virgin Mary. It is doubtful whether the early missionaries were aware, but there were similarities between the myth of Kerrid and the reality of Mary, but it was only after yet more research that Dr Pollard became aware of this.

Although a devout Catholic, Dr Pollard was still a lover of "gods, mythology and all that." In fact she believed that it was they, who had led her into what she called the "one true church", for it was only in the Catholic Church that she found the same romance and mysticism. The difference was that in the Church, God revealed himself without any doubt, whereas myths were just that - purely fictitious narratives involving supernatural persons. Nevertheless she had a belief, which she kept to herself, because it would have been difficult at the time for others to accept, that all religions have and have had a modicum of truth in them. She believed that religious plurality in the world was part of an overall picture. She felt that the knowledge of God was like a vase, which she likened to a '*Babel Vase*,' smashed at the time the Bible chronicles Adam and Eve's loss of the Beatific Vision. This then she felt, became like a giant jigsaw, with each piece including some of the truth. As generations passed only the Jews kept the knowledge of the one true God. Nevertheless God was still the Father of "all nations" (Isaiah), though the majority of the world's people did not know Him, for who He really was, He still cared and provided for them. He made himself known in the innermost soul of people from every culture. As they contemplated with fear and wonder the elements, the order of creation, the cycle of death and rebirth their spirits grew in understanding of the supernatural. He did not abandon His children. He was there with them, but unrecognised. He loved them. He wanted them for all eternity and He had put in place His plan for the redemption of all humanity and the restoration of harmony in the world.

Dr Pollard similarly believed that if God remained active and present in the world so did the devil, the force for evil, Lucifer, Satan or whatever one liked to call him. She accepted that the tale of the battle of the angels in Heaven was an allegorical one, but if there were good and evil spirits at the time of the creation, she was positive the evil spirits did not just rush off to a place called hell and stay there, they would obviously continue their efforts to lead people astray. She regarded the 'good angels' as God's army or civil service, depending on the work in hand, and the 'bad angels' as the terrorists, out to cause mayhem by infiltrating unnoticed. In particular she believed the evil spirits targeted anyone in authority, who had a particular weakness and exploited it. Anyone trying to evangelise or carry on the work of Christ and the apostles on earth would also be marked out. Those who did nothing and had no potential she believed would be left alone, so praying for priests and leaders was her continuous priority.

True knowledge of God is a gift, which was not available to ancient man or most of the pre-Christian world, but nevertheless everyone is born with free will and is able to choose between good and evil. When good is chosen, as opposed to evil, in any religion or culture, God is followed. When evil is knowingly chosen, He is not.

Men and women throughout the generations have pondered the power behind the sun, the moon and all creation. They could not but come to the conclusion that great powers lay behind these mysteries. In the absence of the knowledge of the one true God, they believed there were many Gods, both good and evil and in order to make sense of their beliefs, they wove stories around them and these became the myths and legends of old and which can be found in some parts of the world even now. Those who study these stories (and Dr Pollard was one of them) are often surprised at the similarities of stories to be found in different continents and in completely different cultures. Dr Pollard's conclusion was that the myths and legends were inspired by good or evil spirits (or angels as some prefer to call them), depending on whether they wanted to lead or mislead. She believed that hidden in all beliefs there is a part of the jigsaw puzzle which makes up the truth, and that Christ came to draw all the pieces together again - to rebuild the vase. What she delighted in doing, after having received the gift "of most of the whole picture" as she put it, was to dissect the old myths and decide which parts came from God and which from the devil, whose existence she certainly did not deny, but with whom she wanted nothing to do. She searched through the stories, discovering how many rays of the truth could be found in each 'jigsaw piece.'

When therefore she started to uncover the myth of Kerrid in Cornwall, her interest knew no bounds. Unlike other myths with common themes, Kerrid seemed to be different. She was known as the goddess of love and eternal youth - not the hedonistic desire for youth today, but the eternal youth of immortal life. She was not thought to be powerful of herself, but to rely on a higher spirit, which she accessed via her cauldron, which was her well. In some notes, made on the subject at the time (which still exist in her own hand), Dr Pollard wrote:

CERRID (Cerridwen) the White Lady
Cerrid, patron of Liskeard (her lily in the borough seal) is the owner of the "Cauldron of inspiration and knowledge and renewal of youth. (R Graves, "The White Goddess") In mediaeval times MARY took over Cerrid's cauldron as the fountain of christian inspiration- Ladye Park was the focus of Cerrid's cult in the west and her well was the CAULDRON, corresponding to the HOLY GRAIL. It is called "The sweet cauldron of the five trees." CERRID-WEN means White or Happy Cerrid - LISKEARD derives from LYS KERRID, the Court of Cerrid.

The well did, eventually, officially fall into disuse. The Christian missionaries had introduced the Cornish people to Mary, not a myth but a true human, a woman, born body and soul into this world, now reigning glorified as Queen of Heaven. Because of her unique position as Mother of God, a shrine to her under the name of "Our Lady of the Park" developed. It is likely however that the veneer of Christianity remained quite thin for a long time among the country folk, who under their acceptance had a deep sense of superstition and Kerrid had been part of their lives for generations. Whilst they had the mystique of the Mass, incense, holy water and Mary as a Mother figure their inner spiritual needs were satisfied, but when the Reformation came and all this was banished the English church could not satisfy their deep emotional need. Most did not even understand the English as they only spoke Cornish, but they were obliged to attend services, which were meaningless and empty to them. Locals were forbidden to worship openly in Catholic ways at Our Lady's shrine and according to the records her chapel was dissolved. It is likely that age old memory stirred at this time and locals began visiting the well once more. At a later date it must have fallen into disuse again, for in the records at the Royal Institute of Cornwall, Dr Pollard found a couple of lines referring to the rediscovery of Kerrid's Well in the early 20th century.

"When the well was rediscovered it was found to be full of pins, having been plainly in use for wishing."

It was a custom to throw pins into the well when asking Kerrid's intervention and it is likely that even if this practice stopped for a time, it was restarted once they felt deprived of well loved rituals. The result would have been rather as happens in parts of Africa and South America today, where traditional religions and customs can be found mixed with Christianity.

Records from 13th to 15th centuries showed that the chapel and pilgrimage spot were situated in a clearing between two woods. One was a royal deer park and the other an ordinary thicket. It was from these two woods that the nearby village of 'Doublebois' took its name. In the clearing there was also a royal hunting lodge and it was the king who was responsible for looking after the chapel and shrine and also for appointing the chaplains. This was indicative of how important the centre was deemed to be. It is not known how far back the royal connections stretch, so one can only speculate, but it is very probable that such an important ancient site of religious significance would previously have been patronised by Cornish warlords. Carew writing in the seventeenth century asserted that Liskeard was the seat of Caradoc, Duke of Cornwall in 443 AD.' Dr Borlase who wrote a century later referred to two kings of the same name and on the road from the village of St. Cleer to Liskeard can be seen "King Doniert's Stone." This is a cross base which was found in a pit, near a cross shaft. The cross base has knot decoration of the 9th century and an inscription in Latin. The stone has been set up where it was found, and is thought to refer to a King Doniert who was drowned in AD 878. The fact that it was erected to his memory, so near Liskeard would point to his having frequented the area. Even the legendary King Arthur has connections nearby with King Arthur's Downs and King Arthur's Hall on Bodmin Moor.

All that is left of the royal park today is the wooded hill, which is still part of the Ladye Park Estate. It is documented that archaeological finds of great interest were found there at the beginning of the 20th century, but there seems to be no record of exactly what these were.

Although Dr Pollard had started this research with the idea of presenting a case to Cornwall County Council in order to get the new A38 route changed, she now felt the need to investigate further afield and to discover how originally the myth of Kerrid came to Cornwall.

This investigation led to an even more exciting discovery. Kerrid seemed to be linked to the Cretan Bee Goddess Ker, sometimes spelt Car or Q're, She was a goddess of death and life. Like Shiva the Hindu god of destruction and rebirth, Ker gave both the sting of death and destruction and the honey of love, which leads to new life. It is honey that keeps the hive alive during the long destructive reign of winter and brings it safe into Spring. From fermented honey is made mead, which in ancient days was considered to be the drink of gods and poets, but what excited Dr Pollard most was finding pieces of the jigsaw of truth within the story. It is through bodily destruction and death in this life that we are transformed into a new life of love and immortality.

Bees had always held a fascination for Dr Pollard and at one time she had kept a hive. She had a habit of noting down ideas, which came to her at odd times, and when looking after the bees she had what she called "the honeycomb Idea." It was:

The church as a honeycomb, me or you as a cell - a self-contained unit, full of grace (or maggots) It has no effectual existence apart from comb but perfectly complete in itself"

This thought came back to her, though she had written it long previously, as she read of the connection between Kerrid and Ker. She also could not help but think back to the strange situation of the farmer still living in only half the farm house at Ladye Park with bees living in the other half on the very site that the mythological Kerrid had been honoured. This set her reflecting on her previous view that both good and evil forces are still at work in the world, trying to lead or mislead. She had the thought that although honey is health giving and a God given natural cure for many ills, today many people take royal jelly and pollen tablets as aids to rejuvenation which, though not bad in itself, could be the first step to man believing that he, not God has the control over life and death. She came to the conclusion that before Ladye Park returned to being a shrine to Our Lady, she would need to convert the bees and persuade them to produce Christian honey!

As an historian Dr Pollard knew that the Mediterranean civilisations traded in Cornish tin from the very earliest times and a Cretan axe had been found engraved on Stonehenge. The true Cornish people today, with their swarthy appearance, still bear strong traces of a Mediterranean origin as anyone will vouch, who has visited both Crete and Cornwall. The myth of Ker or Kerrid must have been brought to these islands in the far-off days of Knossos and the great days of Crete. It is not unlikely that the curious spirals one finds in ancient megalithic tombs represent Kerrid as the rings on the abdomen - the womb - of a queen bee.

The more well known mythical gods and goddesses normally had more than one great shrine, and in Devon there appears to be evidence of another centre of the Kerrid cult. The little Devon town of Crediton was in far-off Saxon times the site of a cathedral that was later transferred to Exeter. As Exeter had always been the capital city of the South West, though under different names, there seems to be no reason for the establishment of a cathedral in Crediton, unless it had already been considered a holy place. As it was the Church's policy to convert pagan centres into Christian shrines, she was not surprised to discover that in the early days the town was called *"Kredington"* by the Saxons; in their language *"the town of the children of Kred"* - presumably the followers of Kerrid. Another link which she discovered was that the ancient fairs or feasts of both Liskeard and Crediton were on the same very significant day, September 21st, the eve of the Autumn equinox, after which the nights are longer than the days. It is in Autumn that the honey is collected and all the abundant fruits of the earth showered on mankind by the Creator. It is also in Autumn that the first stings of approaching winter are felt.

The small town of Callington, not far from Liskeard still has a "Honey Fayre" each year whose history must also be connected with Ker.

Glastonbury, in the Somerset marshes also seems to have been a centre for the myth of Kerrid. According to legend, the Holy Grail is hidden within Chalice Hill, from which issues a stream of blood red water. Interestingly there is another legend linking the Holy Grail to the mysterious Dozmary Pool on the edge of Bodmin Moor near Liskeard. She wondered how and why this same Christian subject should be connected to two Kerrid centres.

Kerrid as the intercessor with mother earth seems to have become the leading belief amongst the Brythonic celts, especially in the south west, where they were originally only a small ruling minority, though their language spread through the whole population.

Dates given by scholars for the coming of the Brythonic Celts vary wildly, but 750 BC about the time of the foundation of Rome is a very good average. In South West Britain, the Dumnonian kingdom was set up very early, embracing the present day Cornwall, Devon and Somerset up to the marshes around Glastonbury. Its position made it easily defensible from attack by land and it was in touch with the great world of the South. The Greek traveller Pytheas, who visited Dumnonia on a voyage to Ultima in 300 BC, remarked that its people were very friendly to strangers. A little later Ptolemy, in the world's first universal geography, mentioned the four great towns of Dumnonia – Isca (the capital), Uxella, Voliba and Tamra.

The coming of the Romans many centuries later did not disturb the tenor of Dumnonian life, for they were looked upon as allies against fierce Belgic tribes which had invaded Britain not long before then, and which had already begun to threaten Dumnonia's western frontier. Proudly the capital was renamed ISCA DUMNONIORUM by the Romans and Dumnonia retained internal autonomy under her ancient princes rather like a "native state" in the old British Indian Empire. Inscriptions show that Dumnonian auxiliaries took over the manning of part of Hadrian's Wall far to the north.

When the Romans left in AD400 the only difference to Dumnonia was that she was now fully responsible once more for her own defence. Her geographical position protected her from the Irish, Pictish and Saxon hordes which ravaged most of Britain - no doubt her inhabitants were grateful that that their hive had been protected for so many centuries. At the beginning of the eighth century AD more than three hundred years after the departure of the Romans, Dumnonia was still firmly set in her ancient boundaries of over fifteen hundred years standing. Her king Geraint was addressed by the Saxon Abbot Aldhelm as "The most Glorious Lord of the West".

Aldhelm was trying to persuade King Geraint to persecute those he regarded as pagans and heretics, as was happening in other parts of the country. King Geraint saw no reason to upset his country's long established religious traditions which manifested themselves in a highly individualistic Celtic church, which suited his people very well, but in 710 AD King Nunne of Sussex and King Ine of Wessex led their war hordes into Dumnonia. The long centuries of security were over.

In the genocidal struggle that followed, the Saxons advanced as far as the Hayle estuary, only a few miles from Lands End. When all seemed lost, the Dumnonians rallied and drove them back to the River Tamar, but two thirds of the Kingdom was lost including high-towered Isca. The population was largely dead or had fled across the sea to Brittany. This Cornish remnant of Dumnonia survived for another two hundred years, aided later by the Danes with whose aid it even tried to recapture the lost territories. But their united armies were crushed by the West Saxons at the Battle of

Hingston Down in AD.838. The Cornish rump finally lost its independence when Howell its king was defeated at the Battle of Boleit by King Athelstan of Sussex in AD 936

Howell means 'the sun', and with him the sun of Dumnonia seemed finally to set. Kernewek, the Cornish language continued to be spoken until almost the 19th century and no doubt the myth of Kerrid was frequently invoked in it long after her shrine was suppressed. Discovering all this, Dr Pollard also mused with interest on the fact that both 'Kernewek' and Kerrid begin with the same three letters KER.

Drawing of the statue of Our Lady of the Portal, by Margaret Pollard

Chaptra Hwegh

(Chapter Six)

Kowethas Maria Winn a'n Porth a dhassorgh dhe vywnans

Guild of Our Lady of the Portal springs to life

Researching the history of Ladye Park had been a fascinating exercise for Dr Pollard, more so than she would have dreamed. She found herself going off into flights of fantasy, imagining herself being present in the environs of the site in each of the different centuries, living the life of the pilgrims who would have descended the Mass Path in each generation or watching the dignitaries and their entourages who would have visited in the Middle Ages.

However, she realised that the trunk roads department at County Hall would only be interested in hard facts. Any proof she gave to show the importance of the site would need to be backed up by easily available references, but she also realised that the roads committee would be made up of busy members, who would not want to read more than two pages at most. They would need to be persuaded of the need to re-open the plans without having to spend time checking facts. She therefore decided to condense all she had discovered into two pages of foolscap and instead of referencing quotes she typed out in full on a separate sheet various extracts, which she felt were particularly specific.

The quotation sheet was headed

References showing the historical importance of Ladye Park in Liskeard and supporting an appeal to have the new A38 diverted around it

FROM 'ESSAYS IN CORNISH HISTORY' Charles Henderson

"At Liskeard as at Lanteglos, there were two Duchy parks near together, the old and the new. The latter was more often called Ladye Park from a hunting lodge standing in it. In 1302 the manor of Liskeard contained two woods (hence Double-bois) one park with deer and another without deer. In 1337 Liskeard Park had 200 deer, and in 1353 Robert Wisdom was made its parker with a salary of 2d a day. The old park of Liskeard which lay nearest the town on the west side, contained a chapel of Our Lady, served by a couple of hermits nominated by the dukes. The place where it stood is called LADY PARK - ie Our Lady of the Park" (About 1540 Henry VIII disparked and converted it into cattle pasture)

FROM 'A COMPLETE PAROCHIAL HISTORY OF THE COUNTY OF CORNWALL compiled from the best authorities and corrected and improved from actual survey' Vol III Truro,

William Lake, Boscawen St

London

John Camden Hotten, Piccadilly   1870

LISKEARD

By an Act of 1 Edward VI (1547) for the suppression of chapels, chantries, obits, and other endowments for superstitious uses, the land and property held in trust for them was forfeited to the crown and commissions were issued to enquire what lands and property were so held.

Report of commission relative to this parish:-

"A chapel of our Ladye called Parke in ye town of Lyskeard-Certen lands given to ye said chappell, a garden with an orchard, and half one halfe acre of grounds. And in the said chappell was great oblations some tyme. The yerelye value of ye land xs"

****

The chapel of Our Lady in the Park of Liskeard is often mentioned in the records of the See, and appears to have been frequented by devotees. A garden, an orchard, and half an acre of ground, valued at 10s a year, are recorded to have been given to this chapel. In it were also great oblations which had been contributed at different times. In 1310 it was determined that the vicar had no right to these oblations.

An indulgence dated November 1, 1441, was granted by Bishop Lacy to penitent persons contributing to repair the way to it. There is also a hermitage near the chapel.

****

Henry VII 1487. Mr William Jane was to have, with the consent of the Mayor and Commonality, the next vacancy of "the chapel of the blessed Mary do Old Park." It appears from documents in the Land Revenue Record Office, London that "the chapel of our Lady Park' two acres of land was quoted by deed from Edward VI, 1549 - 60, to Thomas Pomery and Hugh Pomery in fee. The copse below which the chapel was situated is still called Lady Park Wood and many architectural fragments and a good well were discovered there about forty years ago. A neat cottage has been erected on the site by Mr Carthew."

The following more particular extract is from the chapels and chantries Roll, kept at the Record Office.

"A chapel of Our Ladye called Parke in the said town of Lyskerd. Certain lands given to the said chapel; a garden & orchard, and one half acre of ground; and in the said chapel was great oblation some time. None in-cumbent there. The value of the lands belonging to the said chapel Xs. Ornaments none. The number of ounces of plate and jewels is ix ounces. A bell weighing by estimation 1 cwt."

****

The notes were duly passed on to Mr Riche and then Dr Pollard started praying! What Mr Riche did with them and to whom he spoke, she was never quite sure, but on the 10th April 1957 came the news which Dr Pollard had been confident would come. The route of the new A38 had been changed on account of Ladye Park being a site of historical importance. Her joy knew no bounds, but unfortunately this success marked the end of good fortune with reference to the quest to re-establish the shrine.

A question which revolved in both Mr Riche's and Dr Pollard's minds was whether Mr Kelly, the farmer, had been aware of the new road proposals even before their negotiations and whether his wish to purchase the reversion was so that he could then claim far more in compensation from the trunk roads dept when the farm was taken over. Dr Pollard also wondered whether this was the reason that nothing had been heard from the Carthew family in New Zealand. On balance Mr Riche came to the conclusion that both these surmises were unlikely as he had known nothing about it himself until the council meeting. They decided therefore, now that Ladye Park was safe from destruction, to ignore mention of the new road and to continue with plans one way or another to re-open the ancient shrine.

The original meeting, which had been planned with Mr Kelly to discuss renting the shrine site, had been cancelled when the new road scare appeared, but it was now decided to try and re-open negotiations to purchase it. This time Mr Kelly seemed to be very amenable to the idea, but he could not give a price. A valuer was called in again, but Mr Kelly refused to give a price until he knew what rent or amount for the lease would be offered. He doubtless believed that as Dr Pollard was so keen to get hold of the land, it must be very valuable. He would obviously have just kept pushing the price up and up. The irony was that Dr Pollard was so keen to obtain the shrine, she would have paid anything but as no-one could decide a price the negotiations were stalemate.

Then yet another obstacle raised its head. Mr Riche discovered that a covenant existed forbidding religious worship at Ladye Park. At first Margaret Pollard could hardly believe the news. The only reason she was attempting to purchase was to encourage the re-establishment of devotion at the spot. However, she remained undaunted: problems were merely situations to overcome as far as she was concerned, so her first task was to find out whether this covenant could be lifted. It turned out that the covenant would lapse when the lease ended in 1965. She was convinced that it was no coincidence that Our Lady of the Park had expressed a wish to return so near to the restriction coming to an end.

Questions began to form in Margaret's mind. Had the covenant been in existence since the Reformation? If so why had it been placed for so long? She felt the situation could only point to the spot having been such a popular place of pilgrimage that there was no other way to stop the pilgrims, than to forbid them to worship anywhere on the site. She wondered whether an attempt had also been made to even remove memory of the shrine from history, which could well have happened if there had been a return to Kerrid worship after Our Lady's shrine had been dissolved. She also wondered whether a curse had been put on the site. She decided that whatever the answers, she would press on, even more determined to fulfil Our Lady's request.

For the next ten years and more Dr Pollard remained focussed on her belief that she had been given a mission to re-establish the shrine and she did all in her power to do so but it was as though some invisible sinister force was fighting against her all the time. It was not only thwarting her attempts at every turn, but also seemed intent on discrediting the idea in everyone else's mind. Thirty years later she was questioned about these events and she replied in a letter:

"Now as to what happened - We kept getting it in the bag and it kept slipping out. They could find no deeds and the boundary was unknown - Then a weirdo called Anthony somebody, a sort of Father Teresa, who ran the Simon Community, offered to run it as a nursing home for mental cases and sent down two "brothers" who were in fact paramours and one got arrested for indecent exposure. After costing me a small fortune they fled to Walsingham where they set up as Holy Hermits and got a big reputation. Then came a fake "Benedictine" but at this point the parish priest of Liskeard wrote to the bishop and told him if he had the least idea what went on at Ladye Park he would not touch it with a proverbial barge pole. The bishop who had been interested ran away screaming."

She then went on to explain that throughout this time she had continued her research into the history of the shrine and on the very day the parish priest of Liskeard had written to the bishop, she had been reading an essay of Charles Henderson about Ladye Park. She found a footnote about a fraternity of Our Lady of the Portal in Truro. Immediately it struck a chord and she said to herself there and then:

"I've given this thing a good go. It doesn't seem to be getting anywhere. I can only think Our Lady wanted me to light the spark to ignite at some future date. I've done everything in my power. It's now up to Our Lady. If she wants Ladye Park she will arrange it. All the money and effort we have been putting in could be far more gainfully used to re-establish the medieval Fraternity of Our Lady of the Portal and we'll make its express purpose that of building a new church in Truro."

And that is what she did. From that moment she stopped all research into the Liskeard shrine and turned her energies to Truro. Ever since her move from the wonderful Truro Cathedral to the little Catholic chapel twenty years previously, she had dreamt of seeing her Lord in a more prestigious building, quite apart from the obvious need for more space, particularly in the summer months when tourists flocked into Cornwall. Fr Wharton, the parish priest of Truro, was delighted with the idea. He said he thought the greatest miracle would be if Dr Pollard could get back the original £600 she had lodged for the Ladye Park cause, but the bishop was in favour of the idea and that was no problem. Winifride Wharton, Fr Wharton's sister vowed to Our Lady half of any surprise money she might receive and promptly inherited £5000. Dr Pollard's money had been an aunt's legacy and now this amount had arrived, so Our Lady did indeed seem to be paving the way. In fact unlike Ladye Park, this was a project, which went without a hitch from beginning to end. Against all odds more money continued to roll in until there was very quickly enough to employ an architect, purchase a site and start building.

True to form Dr Pollard had already done her research, this time on the Guild of Our Ladye of the Portal and discovered that the original medieval fraternity church had been situated in St Austel Street in Truro. Within no time a very suitable site became available in that very street. Dr Pollard liked to think it might have been on the very same spot, but no records could be found to prove this either way.

The church was to be built on an overgrown piece of ground which had been the garden of an old house. As often happens in these situations many beautiful plants and flowers could be seen struggling for life amongst the brambles. A clump of irises particularly attracted Dr Pollard as she passed the site each morning on her way to Mass at the old chapel for her glorious meeting with Jesus in the Eucharist. When the time came for the bulldozers to move in, she vowed she would dig up the blooms and take them to her own small garden. She could not bear the thought of them being destroyed by heavy machinery, so on the Sunday evening before work was due to begin on the Monday she took her trowel and a bowl and set about extricating them. She had barely begun when she struck something hard. At first she thought it was a stone so began to dig around it. Using her other hand to ease it out she was flabbergasted to discover that in her hand was not a stone, but a larger than life-sized pottery head of a lamb. It looked as though it had broken off from its body, but as there was no sign of any other pieces she carried on digging up the irises and took them and the strange head back home.

The next morning, as usual, she walked past the new site, saying the rosary on her way to 7am Mass. As she walked past the spot, where she had pulled up the irises the previous evening, she noticed that the ground seemed very wet. Walking over to take a closer look, she noticed that there seemed to be a pool of water at the spot.

"Good Gracious" she thought, "I must have burst a pipe when digging up those flowers. I'd better get on to the surveyor."

Returning home after Mass, she immediately phoned the architect, instead, who she knew personally and said:
"You'll never guess what I've gone and done. I think I've cracked a pipe while pinching some irises from the church site. It happened last night but there is a pool of water there now."

"Impossible," came the reply, "A complete survey has been made. There are no pipes on the land. It must be water from the river or somewhere else."

"That's the first time I've heard of water flowing up hill," she retorted, "and we've had no rain for yonks. I think it must be a spring."

"Impossible!" came the reply again "We even employed a water diviner."

"You'll have to come and have a look for yourself, is all I can say, because the workmen are due to start any minute."

Reluctantly the architect agreed to meet her on site half an hour later. Not stopping to lock her door, which she rarely did anyway, she rushed back to St. Austel Street, where a group of labourers were already assembled. The architect arrived at almost the same time and they both walked over to the spot in question. Then as Dr Pollard and the architect stood over the pool, which seemed even larger than two hours before, there was a gurgle and a "whoosh" and up bubbled a spring of water!" They were dumbfounded. The incident had been witnessed by all the workmen who were still standing around awaiting the day's instructions.

At last the architect found his voice:

"This is bang in the middle of where the church is planned. We'll have to try and divert it, but at this moment I can't quite think how."

"No fear" came the instant response. "If it has sprung up just here, that's where Our Lady wants it. We must make it into a well, a new holy well for Cornwall and incorporate it into the church"

And that is exactly what did happen. The water from it was used by Bishop Restieaux of Plymouth in blessing the church at its dedication on Thursday May 17th 1973. A lid of Cornish slate was decided upon, on which was inscribed FONS MARIAE MATRIS PASTORIS ET AGNI (the well of Mary, Mother of the Shepherd and the Lamb). This was partly a quotation (Hail Mother of Lamb and Shepherd) from the Akathistos of the most Holy Mother of God, a hymn in honour of Our Lady of the Portal and translated from Church Slavonic by Margaret Pollard and partly remembering the strange lamb's head that was found just above the spring.

The well with its engraved slate lid can still be found to the left of the altar in the church of Our Lady of the Portal in Truro. Most people are unaware of its existence and the story of how it came to appear is gradually being forgotten.

Gwynsow koynt
Strange winds

It is not known exactly when the term "Lost Shrine of Liskeard" was coined. It came partly from the fact it had lain lost and unknown for so many years, and partly because it was so difficult to find by car, even when one had the address. Originally Dr Pollard called it the "Obstacled shrine'" as so many blocks seemed to be in the way of re-opening it. On one occasion in the late 1950s she and Mr Riche were driving to Ladye Park and suddenly a huge lorry swept into the road ahead. It held them up for miles and miles. Its number was 666, the number of the BEAST in Revelations. To Mr Riche's amusement she announced,

"I don't like the look of that. It seems like an omen that we will lose the battle."

It seemed as though the battle was indeed lost, now that Dr Pollard had turned her attention to Truro, but Ladye Park refused to die down completely. Over the next few years it kept on "rearing its head" to use her own words. Every now and then "unknown interested parties" would ring up and ask her for details from her research and then sheer off again. In September 1969 the Cornish Gorsedd was held in Liskeard and she had a feeling that something might come of that - but nothing did. She was a Cornish bard herself and had been present at the Cornish Gorsedd on Bodmin Moor in 1938. She had taken the name Arlodhes Ywerdhon - "The Irish Lady" after the rock off the Cornish coast. She had also been the Gorsedd harpist. In 1969 nothing remarkable happened as far as she was concerned.

Then in March 1970 Mr Kelly contacted her to say that the solicitor had completed all documents, that everything was ready and he wished to see Mrs Pollard as soon as possible. A very cryptic note was sent back to him, saying he should have done so fifteen years ago. It was too late now.

By 1978 the by-product of the original enterprise, the Fraternity of Our Lady of the Portal had flourished for 13 years and bought the site of the new church of the Portal. It had contributed £1000 a year over a period of years to the church building fund and set on foot a vigorous movement for Unity in Truro. Kate Pollard (as she began to be known at this time) was still a great lover of all things Russian, particularly Russian spirituality, so she was delighted when the fraternity initiated the public recitation of the Akathistos of Our Lady of the Portal in the Truro shrine. Membership grew to include people all over the world. Two religious orders in South Africa were even enrolled and a regular correspondence was established with them.

A fellow parishioner and Dr Margaret Pollard decided the time had come to write a booklet on the history of the Guild of Our Lady of the Portal. They both realised no history would be complete without at least a mention of the ancient shrine of Our Lady of the Park, which would have been in existence at the time of the original medieval guild. It was referred to as the "Strange and romantic shrine of Our Lady in the Park, Liskeard"

Extract from "The Guild of Our Lady of The Portal" by Dr Margaret Pollard and Faith Godbeer, published by Dyllansow Truran Redruth Cornwall

This long forgotten shrine is in the grounds of a farm house and consists of a baptistery with a stream flowing through it and a well, formerly enclosed in a fine well house, whose water has always supplied the farm. The well goes back to pre-Christian times when Liskeard was the centre of devotion to the goddess Kerrid (Liskeard is LYS CERRID) - a kind of Celtic Venus, connected with the Cretan goddess Ker, a death goddess who appears in the form of a bee. A swarm of very aggressive bees infested the farmhouse and could never be got rid of. In Christian times the shrine was made over to Our Lady, and two priests were in charge of it, appointed not by the church but by the Crown; and in the time of Queen Isabella, the "She-Wolf of France," it is likely that a diabolical cult became connected with it, under the control of a bishop - reputed to be a Prince-Bishop Palatine, of valid but highly irregular orders."

Unfortunately no records can be found as to where the information about Queen Isabella and Prince-Bishop Palatine was found, but it is very probable that it was discovered by the mariologist Martin Gillett, who had been so interested in the shrine in the 1950s and early 60s. Unfortunately, although he compiled a file full of notes and wrote various articles to submit for publication he was frightened away from the project by a couple of inexplicable incidents.

Both events happened in the early 1960s. On the first occasion Martin Gillett was researching Ladye Park in the Bodleian Library Oxford. Suddenly there was a bang, a window was blown open with such force that it broke, as a very cold mini whirlwind swept through the room and out a window on the far side. It blew papers everywhere, some flew straight out the window. The library was full at the time and everyone was either stunned or petrified by this eerie experience. Martin Gillett looked at the table where his papers had been and every single one of them had gone. They were his Ladye Park research papers which had been blown out of the window.

Undaunted he started his work again and was back in the library for the next few weeks. There were no more whirlwinds, but for safety sake he made sure that everything he wrote was in a heavy file which could not possibly be blown away and, not wanting to lose his valuable research by unwittingly leaving it on a train or some such, he religiously transferred all notes each night into a brief case, which he kept in his study at home. One evening as he was nearing the end of that particular line of research, he returned to his house as usual, opened his front door without noticing anything untoward and walked straight into his study as was his custom. The site which met his eyes made him stop dead in his tracks. His room had been ransacked. Files from his filing cabinet were strewn all over the floor, books from a bookcase lay untidily heaped on the table beneath it and every cupboard was open. When however he began to check to see what had been stolen, he found the only thing missing was his brief case containing the Ladye Park notes. He had an uncomfortable feeling that this was not an ordinary break in. This he felt was the result of some supernatural force and not a good one, which did not want Our Lady honoured with the re-establishment of her shrine or the development of a new one. He later hinted that the research he had been doing had uncovered an earlier battle of good and evil at the site, but that light had overcome the darkness as it always does eventually. He wondered whether Our Lady's stirring and the thought of the Blessed Trinity becoming the focus of people's lives once more was too much for 'the evil one' and there was a determination to stop any Christian revival. At the time Martin Gillett said that this should make us all the more determined to pray for any obstacles to be overcome, so that joy could replace sadness in people's lives and that Mary and her Blessed Son could once more be glorified at the spot, but it was shortly after this that he began to lose interest in further research and never published any of the articles he had written. We can only guess, what went through his mind and whether other incidents made him feel it was best to leave well alone.

Some time later when Kate Pollard was speaking of the number of people the devil seemed to have attacked to stop Our Lady's wish coming true, she said,

"I don't seem to have been attacked yet. I think it would be jolly exciting if I was. I'd pull out all the stops, drawing on every grace available from the Sacraments and the rosary to defeat him. The rosary is a sure flattener. He hates that! However the old goddess (I believe the devil is sometimes male, sometimes female and sometimes neuter) knows how to attack those without suitable armour like the Trewithens. They suffered vandal attacks, illness, the wrath of the bees - even their attempt to run a shop in Liskeard went bust. I was despondent. I prayed the rosary like mad but sometimes the curse is so entrenched it needs the person concerned to pray the rosary too "

One of the many hold-ups in the saga of Kate Pollard's attempt to purchase Ladye Park had been the discovery that the land was owned partly by the Carthews and leased to Kelly, partly owned by Kelly himself and partly by his wife and the boundary line between the Carthew's and Kelly's part went straight through the middle of the house. When Mr Kelly had said that all the paperwork had now been completed he was speaking the truth. All three parties had, not without some difficulty, banded together to sell the house and some of the farm. Mr Kelly had decided to retain some of the fields but now that Kate Pollard had given a definite "No", the house and farm was put on the market and sold to a local farmer Mr Mitchell.

Three years later in 1976 the house and one and a half acres of land including the orchard and the shrine were sold again, this time to an American/German couple, John and Ursula Schneider. They did not purchase the farmland, the nearby Gatehouse, or the wooded hill behind the property, though these were all offered to them. Instead they made an offer for the house and garden alone and it was accepted. The whole property had been advertised. The Schneiders arranged to view and fell in love with the house, garden and setting at first sight. They were living in Germany at the time and thought Ladye Park would be ideal for their retirement. They realised soon after purchase something, which many lovers of Cornwall who decide to retire there discover and that is that Cornwall is a   long way from anywhere! They found it took 24 hours to travel from their German home to Liskeard - certainly too long for a weekend break. They then purchased a plane which made travel far easier, as the trip now only took three and a half hours and they then began to spend several long weekends and holidays there. A great deal of money was spent modernising the house, but they loved the spot and so did the many friends who were also invited to visit.

In 1980 their life suddenly changed. Mr Schneider became Vice President of his company and two years later he was transferred to the United States. Trips to Ladye Park were now impossible apart from for summer vacations. They still hoped to keep their "Cornish Jewel" and found excellent caretakers, but from being a joy to them the house began to become a liability. It was very difficult managing a house from so far away and they increasingly began to find that their two weeks annual holiday there was taken up with arranging repairs, and general maintenance around the house and so in 1992 they put the house back on the market for the first time.

Inside the new Truro church

Above: Mrs Pollard (in headscarf) and her pilgrims being
welcomed on the steps to Vierzehnheiligen Basilica

Below: The Duchess of Franconia's tapestry

Chaptra Seyth

(Chapter seven)
Vierzehnheiligen ha Truru
Vierzehnheiligen and Truro

To most people the experience of believing one has been given a specific mission to fulfil and of throwing oneself wholeheartedly into it, only to experience utter failure, would be enough at best to sap their confidence and at worst make them doubt their original sanity. This was certainly not the case for Margaret Pollard. She never doubted Our Lady's message or that she still had Liskeard in mind. As far as she was concerned Our Lady was entitled to carry out her plan as and when she wished. Kate had often said that she was like Moses, given the job of starting things for others to complete. There was absolutely no doubt in her mind that she had been asked to start the ball rolling but she also had no doubt that it was Our Lady's prerogative to stop it rolling for a while if she wished and that was how Kate took the present situation - a time of interval in the game, which would resume in due course. Meanwhile she continued with her many interests, which included church and charitable activities, music, languages, environmental pursuits, books and more.

Needlework had been one of her great hobbies throughout her life, but in the early 1970's she met a young man by the name of Michael, a schoolboy at the time, who recognised her great talent. Up until then she had made some beautiful tapestry kneelers for the church and embroidered anything she could lay hands on. Michael threw out a bet to her that she couldn't make a piece of embroidery longer than the Bayeux tapestry.

"I'll give it a go" she replied, "but what subject should we use?"

Michael suggested the Narnia stories, which at the time she had never even heard of despite having read many other CS Lewis books. When she did read them she was delighted and was thrilled to set to work on the mammoth task, which confronted her. This piece of embroidery ended up 1,338 feet long and was in the Guinness Book of Records as the longest in the world. Many more suggestions from Michael for tapestries followed, each one was larger and more intricate than the one before. Each time she finished one, he would suggest another and she would set to work again. She had always said that she was much happier as a slave carrying out other people's wishes, but even she could not quite understand the almost Svengali hold he had over her. When interviewed on the radio for her eightieth birthday, she was questioned about him and she admitted that she had once written a poem to him questioning her own feelings and motives. It was written in the rather complex form of a ballade (see appendix).

Dr Pollard was constantly being asked for interviews for newspaper articles and radio programmes. A Nationwide TV programme was made about her, but she did not possess a television so never saw it and she was not particularly interested in doing so. She rarely saw the newspaper articles either, usually saying after an interview something like,

"He was such a nice man. I enjoyed talking to him but I can't for the life of me think why he wants to write about me. Still if conversing with me helps him earn his living that's fine by me, especially as I always manage to bring God into conversations somehow, so who knows how many get converted afterwards without me knowing".

Recipients of her avid correspondence found a treat in store every time they opened a letter from her. In the early days they were perfectly typed on the backs of any official correspondence or junk mail, in fact anything which came written on one side only. She wasted nothing, being very aware of the difference in living standards between the 'haves and have nots' and saved every penny she could to pass on to the less fortunate This was in addition to giving away her own not inconsiderable inherited fortune, so that by the time she died she had nothing and was attached to nothing, which was how she wanted it. In her latter years when she had lost her sight and was bedridden, she continued to correspond using black felt-tip pens on brightly coloured yellow Xray paper, which she was obviously given by someone who worked in a hospital. She wrote in capitals surmising that it would more likely to be easier to read than script but she occasionally went off the page or wrote over a page she had already written on. Even if deciphering the contents took a little time it was worth every minute and more. Each letter contained comments on the recipients previous letter (she only corresponded with people who wrote back) and was packed full of thoughts which had come to her, quotations, humorous anecdotes, true or fictitious, theological ideas and statements, which ranged from the sublime to the ridiculous and just anything which came to her. They could sometimes be described as intellectual treatises and sometimes as hilarious rubbish. Sometimes both appeared in the same letter. Her one foible was that she never dated anything, so unless one dated letters oneself on receipt, it was a case of guesswork to know even in what year they were written, when coming across them again at a later date. She also had a habit of referring to women as "judies".

One friend kept a letter which she thinks was written around 1989. After various pleasantries and thanking her for the beautiful ikon of Florence Nightingale (a £20 note donation to her worthwhile causes) Mrs Pollard went on to write

"I played for a Requiem today, a judy nobody seemed to have ever heard of, but there were a lot in church. I want to tell you about an idea that came into my head, you know all these fools who want to make out that God is feminine because they say judies don't get a fair play - well I discovered that GOD is masculine and no two ways about it, TRINITY HOWEVER IS FEMININE IN ALL LANGUAGES- Greek, Latin, Slavonic, all the modern ones, even Cornish and Breton! so there it is, hidden in code as it were so every time you address the Trinity (which incidentally is not found in the Bible) you say SHE Except only in English where we hedge our bets on gender so you take your choice.
TRINITY
Greek -   *Trias*
Latin -   Trinitas

Slavonic - Troitsa
German - Dreifaltigkeit
French - Trinité
Spanish - Trinidad
Italian - Trinità
Cornish _ Trynsys
Breton - Treinded
All Feminine

The other thing is what I consider to be an absolute proof of the existence of God. Try this one on an atheist. God is Truth. Now if there was an absolute Truth that existed before the world was created that would prove the existence of a creative MIND that contained it. There are five solid bodies and no more since before time began, called the Platonic solids. I once made patchwork models of them and hung them up in the window. These existed always in the mind of God and were not invented by man, they had to be discovered. They are the Tetrahedron, cube, octahedron, dodecahedron and   icosahedron. I think of them as a sort of luminous jobs floating in space, it is not possible they could have come together by chance. One might perhaps, or else lots of them, but just five and no more (like the five wounds of Christ, five is decidedly a mystic number) and they were there eternally before anything was created and will be long after we all pack it in. I made an awfully nice dodecahedron (the 12 sided job) out of pentagons which are easy enough to sew together like a patchwork quilt if you have a cardboard template to start with. It's my favourite one and I made up a mental dodecahedron with five-letter words that are all attributes of God, like Mercy, Peace, Light, Glory, Grace, Truth, power, Alpha, Omega the rest escapes my memory for the moment anyway there were twelve in all. Like a sort of space ship.

I remember the twelfth now it was UNITY! Well I thought of this twelve sided job floating in the air slowly turning round showing different aspects of God. Now you see why I don't want the telly! Like the child in Punch who was put in the corner for contumacious conduct defiantly remarked "I don't care. I can fink funny foughts."

On her 80th birthday, 1st March 1984 Margaret Pollard was honoured with a presentation to her of a Benemerenti Medal. This is a very special tribute, awarded by the Pope for lay people, who have made exceptional contribution to their parish or church life, rather like a religious OBE. She said on receipt of it she was "flabbergasted, humbled and at the same time absolutely thrilled" to be the recipient of such an honour.

The local publicity which ensued included her being interviewed for Radio Cornwall. When asked why she had been chosen for the medal, she said she did not know, but she presumed it was something to do with her having been the bulldozer behind getting the new RC church built in Truro. She was then asked how she came to instigate the idea and she replied:

Extract from Interview with Margaret Pollard on Radio Cornwall March 1984
N.B. This interview was given "off the cuff" Dr Pollard having no idea that it would be transcribed or kept for posterity. Consequently her main aim was to amuse and entertain rather than to be historically accurate on every single detail. It is also coloured by her inclination at all times to give others credit rather than herself.

It's a most romantic story. It goes back to a long forgotten shrine of which there are still some remains at Liskeard, called 'Our Lady of the Park' Now this was a royally appointed shrine and it lay between two forests which give the name of Doublebois to that village. You see there was a royal forest and an ordinary forest. They were hunting forests and in between them was a clearing with this shrine in. Then the priests were appointed by the King not by the Church and it was very famous in its day and great offerings were made there and many pilgrimages, but the thing about it is it goes back to far beyond Christian times to the ancient Goddess Ceridwen or Kerrid - the Court of Kerrid. She was the patron Goddess of Liskeard, so the Christian veneer so to speak, was always rather thin there. I think the influence of the old Goddess lasted. It has lasted to this point. We tried for a long time - many years to get the shrine for the church. The bishop was willing to hold it on behalf of the church but we never succeeded. We always ran into every kind of trouble and I had a strong feeling that there was some sinister dark power behind this. Anyway it never succeeded and at last I had been reading in a book of Charles Henderson Essays finding out information about Our Lady of the Park. I said to Fr Wharton who was our parish priest then "Did you know that according to Charles Henderson there was at that time, in the Middle Ages. a very prosperous and powerful Guild of Our Lady of the Portal in Truro?" Fr Wharton said, "Let's drop this Park thing. We'll never get anywhere with it. Lets concentrate on the Portal. We'll build a new church to Our Lady of the Portal and forget all about Our Lady in the Park. We're not going to get anywhere so I said "Right let's" and from that moment the hand of the Lord was with us. Nothing went wrong with this scheme. Fr Wharton, after three botch shots found the ideal site and he went to the agent and asked the price who said "£9,000" (Only think how little that is today - £9000)

He said "I'll want a deposit." Fr Wharton simply plonked the whole purchase price on the table. The agent nearly fainted. He said he'd never known that done before so he secured the site. That money was produced entirely by the newly revived Guild of Our Lady of the Portal, which Fr Wharton had immediately set about doing, and so he bought the site and in due course they began to build the church, and now a really exciting thing happened. They were of course working away with their excavating machines. I used to go down every day and I used to say the rosary on the spot to boost things along. I noticed one day a vast pool of water below where they were to dig. I said to the foreman,
"What's this water? Where does it come from?"
"Oh I think it's probably the tide."
I said "I have yet to learn that water rises above its own level", so then he said,
"If it isn't that it's the drains from the houses at the back." "We can't get rid of it" and so I said

"I think it's a spring."

He said "Oh no, it isn't - not a spring."

By that time we had Fr Lawrence Byrne. Fr Wharton was then Prior, I think, but anyhow Fr Lawrence Byrne was here. I told him about this and he said,

"Oh no, I don't think it's a spring"

He said *"It's surface water"* I said *"I don't think so. We've had a long dry spell and this thing keeps filling up and they pump and pump. It fills up every day"* so then I went and talked to the architect about it and the architect said *"well the only thing we can do is to sort of block the thing off."* I said,

"Oh don't do that. Please don't. I'm sure this is a spring." I said "Come along and look at it "

"So he and I, we went along to the works. There was the foreman and everybody - plenty of witnesses and without a word of a lie as we stood there looking at this thing there was a sort of gurgle and water began to flow right out of the rock. The architect burst out laughing and said,

"It is a spring all right."

In the meantime I had given a bottle of this water to a friend I have who works in Holmans. He got them to analyse this in their laboratory and we got an analysis back saying, "This is typical spring water. I'll tell you all the minerals in it," so there we were and even then they didn't believe, but they believed when they saw the water coming out so the architect said,

"We've obviously got to keep this. We'll make it a feature but you do realise don't you that it's going to be inside the church, and I think I'll put it in a pipe so that it comes up and you can get water out of it, and so he did he fixed it up with a pipe and you can get water out of it for baptisms and all the rest. I said,

"That's grand" - so he did. *he fixed it up with a pipe.*

Just before I had been trying to dig up a clump of irises in the garden of the old ruined cottage. I wanted to save the life of these irises. As I was digging my trowel hit something hard and so I dug carefully round it and out came a most remarkable thing which was a huge great pottery head of a lamb - no sign of a body - just the head of a lamb - a curious thing - bigger than life size. I showed this to Fr Lawrence later and I said,

"I think this proves something. This was where the spring is. It was right on top of it" - and so he said "It's very curious. I'd keep it if I was you. I still don't think it's a spring." When the well was finally in working order Fr Lawrence said to me, "We must have a nice inscribed slate on the top. What do you suggest for an inscription?" I said,

"Could we have something about the lamb? I think the lamb comes into it." and he said ,

"What can you think of?"

Then I thought of a delightful invocation which comes into the Russian hymn to Our Lady called the Akathistos. 'Hail Mother both of lamb and shepherd" so I put it into Latin for him and he had it inscribed on the lid and there it is. THE WELL OF MARY THE MOTHER OF THE LAMB AND SHEPHERD and this as far as I know is the only well in Cornwall dedicated to Our Lady and it has proved of absolute sterling worth. It has never run dry in all these years, not in 10 years and there have been some very dry summers as you know, long spells of drought but the well has never run dry. We've always supplied enough water for baptisms, filling the stoops, consecrating houses and all that kind of thing and I have the honour of getting the water up and I get it up in a pewter mug which belonged to my husband who was a commander of a

minesweeper during the war and the crew of this mine sweeper gave him this pewter mug so it was a sort of souvenir of him so I put this mug on a piece of string and I let it down just like the woman of Samaria - I feel rather like the woman of Samaria when I get the water up and once a terrible thing happened and Pollard's mug came off the string and went down to the bottom and so I thought this is terrible. What shall we do? We can't get it up again - not possibly down that pipe so the secretary at the time, Mrs Gibson, she had a pewter mug herself so she lent me her pewter mug, as I'd got to get water up, so I let her pewter mug down and up it came, and believe me Pollard's mug was clinging to it! They were stuck together and I hoisted both of them up together and I'm using the same mug today still.

The interviewer then went on to ask about her tapestries, particularly the Narnia tapestry, "the longest tapestry in the world." Mrs Pollard explained that it was in reality a piece of embroidery, not a tapestry and she explained how it had come to be in the Guinness Book of Records. She also spoke of the very large tapestry which she was working on at the time entitled the "Duchess of Franconia" which she said was her largest and best and likely to be her last. When asked how she had come to design it she explained how a few years previously she had come across a book on German Baroque architecture. She had never been interested in Baroque art previously, but flipping through this book she suddenly came upon a picture from the basilica of Vierzehnheilligen in Bavaria *"which at first amused me beyond bounds, and then fascinated me. It was the most extraordinary great shrine with a canopy. In fact it looked like a state coach. It was in truth modelled on a statecoach and this was a shrine to the saints known as the 14 Holy Helpers. These were fourteen well known early Christian saints who seemed to provide for every human need, from St Erasmus, patron saint of those with diseases below the belt to St Pantaleon, patron saint of those with neurological illnesses. He is depicted with a nail through his head. Four of the saints were sitting on the roof, two of them were propping up the sides. Four of them were sitting on great huge scallop structures. Half way up, the other four were standing around the edge. You never saw anything funnier in your life or more delightful. I stared at this thing and stared at it. I began by laughing and then made up my mind I wanted to see it."*

Mrs Pollard then went on to explain the wonderful adventure she had with Michael Maine and his friend David, finding out how to get there and making the trip. She had never flown before in her life and gave an amusing explanation of her experiences. The only flight they could get was with Philippine Airlines. The receptionist for the airline went by the delightful name of Cinderella Wang but the plane turned out to be a "venerable Jumbo" which she thought looked "pretty antique" as though it came from a "Jumble Sale". Her fears which had started before even boarding the plane were confirmed, when the Captain after a long delay came over the intercom to say he regretted it, but they would be three hours late in starting due to "Mechanical defects". She started saying the Office of the Dead, making acts of contrition, and preparing herself for the next world. She felt very solemn but hoped she was in a state of grace, when suddenly David said, "We're over the Channel." She could not believe it. She had not realised they had even taken off, so none of the stories she had heard about your entrails being left behind and your ears blowing out had been true. The flight was an absolute joy for her.

When they eventually arrived at Vierzehnheiligen, 200km from Frankfurt, the sight which met her eyes was breathtaking. The shrine was set in a magnificent basilica designed by Balthazar Neuman. It overlooked the valley of the River Maine. As she entered through the large central doors, she saw the sun streaming in on a mass of white, gold and marble. Cherubs were everywhere - on the ceilings, on the walls and around the many statues - and in the middle was the magnificent shrine of the Fourteen Holy Helpers in Times of Distress, which she had seen in the book of Baroque architecture. There and then she thought, "This is Heaven on earth and it's where I want my ashes to lie after my death, but before then I want to go back home and tell all my friends about this place and then to bring them back on a massive Cornish pilgrimage. I want to bring them here because this proves that God is FUN."

On returning home she immediately began two projects, the first to find a travel agent willing to arrange transport of a group to Bavaria and the second the planning and completion of a tapestry. The latter now hangs on the wall of the church of Our Lady of the Portal in Truro. It shows the Coronation of Our Lady with the 14 saints of Vierzehnheiligen. Our Lord (blond and beardless in the style of Sir Ninian Comper) is shown crowning his Mother as Queen of Heaven - they are in a shrine which is copied from the extraordinary shrine at Vierzehnheiligen - below them are grouped the "Holy Helpers in Times of Distress": SS Cyriac, Denis, Guy, Catherine, Barbara (holding a model of Truro cathedral in her lap), Pantaleon, Christopher, Achatius, Margaret, Erasmus, Giles, Eustace, Blaise and George. To the left and right were added Blessed Alain de Solminac, a recently beatified Cannon Regular of the Lateran and St Dominic (her favourite saint). It also featured bees and deer to represent Ladye Park, because she was convinced that one day after her death there would be a link between the three shrines. She did not know what the link would be but she was convinced she had been called to all three for a purpose.

The following year she led the first English pilgrimage ever to Vierzehnheiligen and it was welcomed with a mayoral reception in the nearby small town of Staffelstein. For several years afterwards until she became too old to continue, other annual pilgrimages were also held. One summer the pilgrimage had coincided with the Vierzehnheilligen feast of the 'Duchess of Franconia' - Our Lady of Franconia. It was as she put it "a truly magnificent affair" at the end of wine harvesting, with the most wonderful procession. There were banners carried by all and sundry including one, which she herself made to represent the English contingent. This banner still hangs in the votive room of the basilica, but she knew as she walked in that procession, that although it might be her last visit to Vierzehnheiligen she was meant to go back home and start her largest and best tapestry, featuring "The Duchess of Franconia" This she did.

Above: The re-hallowing of the Shrine in May 1979

Below: Detail from the banner made by Margaret Pollard
for the re-hallowing of the Shrine

Chaptra Eth

(Chapter Eight)
Dassakrans an Grerva
The Re-hallowing of the Shrine

By 1978 everything concerning the shrine of Our Lady of the Park had gone dead. Mrs Pollard had not lost her faith in its future, but there were no signs to encourage her confidence.

In the July of that year a Mrs Joan Praag made contact with the then occupiers of Ladye Park a Mr & Mrs George, who were acting as caretakers for Mr & Mrs Schneider, the German/American owners. She was invited to make a visit, so knowing her interest she asked Margaret Pollard to go along with her. They found the farm beautifully looked after. The Georges were living in the old part of the house that had been the chapel and which had previously lain empty. Without either Mrs Pollard or Joan Praag mentioning it the Georges volunteered that they were having problems because there was an infestation of bees. Just being on the premises brought back all Mrs Pollard's enthusiasm for the place. She started talking nineteen to the dozen about its history and said how wonderful it was that they were living there. She promised on her return to send them a brief résumé of some of her research. This she did immediately on arrival home.

This visit seemed to herald a mini revival of interest in the Marian shrine. In October of that same year Mrs Pollard heard via a friend that the Society of Mary, based at Truro Cathedral was interested in arranging a pilgrimage to Ladye Park. One of their members, a Horace Keast had become very excited because he thought he was the first person in modern times to discover that there had once been a great place of pilgrimage in Liskeard. He had enthused the members to arrange a re-hallowing of the site, so the following year 1979 on 29th May the first pilgrimage since the Reformation took place to the shrine of Our Ladye of the Park. It was an ecumenical pilgrimage organised jointly by the Guild of Our

Lady of the Portal and the Society of Mary. It was led by Anglican Fr Tim Van Carrapiett, priest in charge of St Day. Several other Anglican clergy attended. However, although no Catholic priest was in attendance, it was well supported by Catholic laity, some from as far afield as London. The pilgrimage began with Vespers in Menheniot parish church. All the pilgrims then travelled in private cars to Ladye Park. Assembling in the lane outside, they unfurled their banners. One had been embroidered by Mrs Pollard specially for the occasion. It showed the figure of Our Lady offering a toy deer to the child. This was a reminder of the fact that the shrine stood in a clearing between two forests, one of which was the royal hunting forest. The well, orchard and stream were shown as well as a swarm of bees. The antiphon of the Mass of the Mother of Fair Love, "Come, Our Lady, come, our Queen, into your garden; the scent of your garments is sweeter than all perfumes" was embroidered on the banner.

The procession then slowly wound its way around the site singing the hymns composed specially for the occasion. It ended with a very spiritually moving re-dedication of the shrine by Fr Van Carrapiett and the prayers for Christian Unity also compiled for the pilgrimage.

PRAYERS FOR CHRISTIAN UNITY
Used for first pilgrimage to Ladye Park since the Reformation
29th May 1979

Our help is in the name of the Lord: who hath made heaven and earth.

Let us pray

O God, who art strength unchangeable and Light eternal: look down in mercy on the wondrous mystery of Thy whole Church, and by the operation of Thy continual providence accomplish in tranquility the work of Man's salvation; and let the whole world perceive and know that things cast down are being raised up, things grown old are being made new, and all things are returning to their perfection, through him from whom they took their beginning, Jesus Christ Thy Son Our Lord. Amen

O God, who has commanded us to honour the Blessed Mary Virgin Queen of all the saints, as the Mother of Fair Love: graciously grant that under her protection in this world we may love Thee in all things and above all things and enjoy the blessed company of Thy Saints in heaven. Through Jesus Christ Our Lord   Amen

OUR FATHER   HAIL MARY   GLORIA
Intention Unity

O Lord Jesus Christ who said to Thine apostles, Peace I leave with you, my peace I give unto you: regard not our sins but the faith of Thy Church and vouchsafe to grant her peace and unity according to Thy will: who livest and reignest God throughout all ages, world without end. Amen

OUR LADY OF THE PARK
PRAY FOR US
The service ended with the following:
This, the first pilgrimage and re-hallowing of the site of the shrine of Our Lady in the Park, Liskeard, has been an outward expression of the inward desire of many Christians for a greater degree of UNITY.
We have dedicated this holy place for all time to be a place of ecumenical pilgrimage in Cornwall. We pray that as the ties of friendship deepen and as a material expression of our spiritual desires a permanent shrine may once more be raised where all may come and join together in worship, fellowship and love.
The Blessed Virgin loves above all to see in her children, Purity, Humility and Charity. May these virtues be ours as we seek to re-establish this shrine of UNITY.

Viewing these prayers from the beginning of the 21st century, they will appear to many as archaic in format and wording and yet the words "things grown old are being made new, and all things are returning to their perfection" strikes a chord of optimism at the beginning of a new millennium.

At the time these words were written, moves towards Christian Unity were very much in their infancy and on the whole unity referred to unity between Anglicans and Roman Catholics, but as we stand viewing the new century and millennium before us, our thoughts and ideals and those of the Church have taken a giant step further, for now we think in terms of both Christian unity and interreligious relations. At the time of the 1979 pilgrimage it would have been considered almost sacrilegious to suggest that the pre-Christian religions and many non-Christian religions today have aspects which unite them, but an article by John Borelli Secretary of the American RC Bishops' Conference on Interreligous dialogue in **MONOS** - *A Journal for Those Seeking Spiritual Growth Dec 2000* quotes the encyclical *Nostra Aetate (Our Time)(1997)* and states it accepts that there is "an awareness of a hidden power" in all people and that this is the unity of the human community. The article also says of the encyclical that it, "specifically names Jews, Muslims, Buddhists and Hindus and also notes the "deep religious sense" among all peoples whose way of life is religious."

He then goes on to quote Pope John Paul II from **Redemptoris Missio 1990** which stated very clearly that the Catholic Church not only respects every individual for being open to God and the action of the Spirit, but also understands that God works through other religious traditions. He says the text moves beyond a statement of respect for all religious persons and a belief that all humanity is directed towards God. It states explicitly a respect for religions in themselves because they are means through which God communicates to humanity.

In the light of the above one wonders whether Our Lady purposely delayed the permanent re-opening of her shrine until a time when it could become a true centre of unity where Mary could enfold everyone, no matter what their religious persuasion, in her mantle of peace.

One of the pilgrims, who travelled from London for the

occasion of the re-dedication of the shrine of Our Lady of the Park, was Sister 13 of the Guild of Our Lady of the Portal in Truro. All members of the guild went by numbers instead of their names in order to preserve anonymity. This pampered to Margaret Pollard's lifelong hatred of notoriety and the belief that a name was not for life but a means of being identified for specific occasions or tasks. She herself had a myriad of names besides Dr and Mrs Pollard, Margaret and Peggy - there were also Meg (after Gypsy Meg), Mah (to her South African friends), Sister 10 of the Guild of Our Lady of the Portal, and many more. Sister 13 had been a young teenager in 1955 and had been one of the few who had been privy to the story of the vision and had seen the picture 'La Vierge à la Porcelaine ' before it was sold to Lord St Levan. She had become one of the founder members of the Guild of Our Lady of the Portal, but very soon after had moved to London to study and then work, so her contact with Cornwall began to diminish until she all but lost touch. She heard about the pilgrimage of 29th May 1979 from another family member and decided she would like to attend for old times sake. At this time in her life, she was a church-goer, but would not have described herself as particularly religious. It was a time in her life, when socialising and enjoying life was her priority. She would not have gone so far as to say that religion was irrelevant to her, but nor would she have said that it was her faith which gave her the joy in her life.

Sister 13 travelled to Cornwall via Bournemouth, staying Friday night there with family before travelling on by car on the Saturday. Unfortunately she had not reckoned on the tremendous traffic jams en route, so in spite of having allowed six hours for a four hour journey the starting time of the pilgrimage, 3 pm found her still driving the car on the wrong side of the River Tamar. Suddenly it appeared vital that she should get to Ladye Park on time and she began praying as she had never prayed before.

Whether by luck or divine providence she did not know, but at 3.45 pm she reached Ladye Park, just as the rest of the pilgrimage was arriving from Vespers in Menheniot parish church. Mrs Pollard greeted her immediately and said she had not been a bit worried.

She knew the power of evil would not be able to resist causing a bit of trouble, but God always won in the end. The important part, she said was the procession and Our Lady would not let her miss that. Sister 13 was not so sure, but she was glad she was there. However, as she joined the band of banner and rosary carrying pilgrims, she began to feel awkward and then very embarrassed. Her brand of religion was very personal and not one to wear on her sleeve. She began to wish she had not prayed quite so hard to get there on time. A small crowd of people including Mr & Mrs George, the Ladye Park caretakers at the time and some of their friends were standing at the side watching the procession. Sister 13's main concern was that none of them knew her or recognised her. When a flash from a photographer went off, Sister 13's mortification knew no bounds. What if it ended up in the paper and she was recognised! Still she was here now and so might as well forget her embarrassment and concentrate on the matter in hand, the procession around the site and the service of re-dedication.

As she began to sing the words of the Ladye Park hymn with its chorus "Lady Mary, Blessed Mary, Lady Mary of the Park" she began to relax and enter into the spirit of the pilgrimage and then as she processed, with all the other pilgrims still singing the hymn, from the well to what was thought to be the remains of an altar, where Mass would have been said centuries before, she had an experience which she will remember clearly for the rest of her days. It was, as they say in Cornish *"omglywans na yllir y styra"* (an inexplicable feeling). She suddenly felt a sharp tingle go right through her body, like an electric shock. This was followed by a jolt or jump within her. Then the shock was gone and she was left with a glorious feeling of wonder and joy. It could not have taken more than a few seconds, for no one around her noticed that anything had happened to her. She carried on with the procession still full of the joy but also knowing that something had changed within her. She knew that she was no longer embarrassed to be seen walking in a pilgrimage. In fact it was the opposite she knew she would never be embarrassed again and that somehow she was going to be involved with the future of this shrine.

Before beginning the long drive back to London she wrote her name and address on a piece of paper and handed it to the organisers saying,

"If you have a list of interested parties please add my name to it. I would like to be informed of any future pilgrimages to this shrine. I will gladly refund postage and any costs"

She was told that, now the site had been re-hallowed, one was likely to be organised each year on the last Saturday in May. Sister 13 drove off happy with this knowledge, but she was not notified the following year or the one after that because there were none. Fr Van Carrapiett the Anglican priest who had been the mainstay in the organisation "upped and went" to Brighton soon after and consequently lost interest. Presumably the Society of Mary could not find a replacement and so the spark of interest died down once more.

Ten years later notes made at the time of the pilgrimage by Howard Jewell, who was made a bard of the Cornish Gorsedd in 1944 and was in attendance, were found and transcribed by M A Orchard, one time President of the Old Cornish society, who gave permission for them to be included here.

....

Transcribed from C H Jewell's notes 1979 by M A Orchard
Ladye Park Well, Liskeard
In the 16th Century a little shrine and hermitage was closed in the pleasant vale of 'Our Lady of the Park' Liskeard. Many hearts were surely sad and afraid. The small chapel was stripped, the Chalice confiscated, the bell doubtless became scrap metal. No one dared to complain or ever mention the sad affair. Altar and statue destroyed the shrine slowly gathered moss and mould and now scarcely a trace remains of a once revered Holy and Hallowed place. The deer nibbled the lush grass a while longer and finally the pleasant grove was disparked, its shy inhabitants removed or eaten!
On the last Saturday of Our Lady's month, the month of May (1979) time once more took its subtle revenge. Lovers of Mary have been carefully recreating the Cornish past - Peggy Pollard and Horace Keast, both of Truro, have independently pursued the

history of 'Our Lady's chief shrine in Cornwall'.

The Guild of 'Our Lady of the Portal' and the Anglican "Society of Mary" led by Father Timothy van Carapiett combined together on Pilgrimage on a pleasant Spring afternoon reverently reviving and restoring honour to Blessed Mary in the green pasture and woodland.

It was a very simple ceremony - preceded by Solemn Vespers of Our Lady in the stately Parish Church of Menheniot at which 40 people were present, Anglican and Roman.

After tea in the Church Hall Mr Horace Keast recited the litany of "Our Lady of the Park" with comments by Mrs Pollard who identifies the well there with the cults of a Pagan water Deity, Ceridwen, from which Liskeard - Court of Cerrid - may derive.

The possibility of reviving the shrine was discussed, certainly pilgrimages will now take place annually. The miracle of the Walsingham revival comes to mind, with God nothing is impossible.

Then the procession of cars sped along the Liskeard by-pass to the site of Our Lady Park, down in the valley below. A hymn had been composed for the Pilgrimage and this was sung as the thurifer (C.H.Jewell) led the robed clergy and pilgrims to a cascading fountain making a station for prayer. Then to the re-hallowing of the splendid well, which is reached down a flight of steps, a small niche of ancient origin was censed with a prayer, and finally a stop at the hedge of the shrine where the owner of Ladye Park welcomed us. These bald statements cannot convey the atmosphere of sanctity and peace and powerful action of 'doing' the pilgrimage.

Fresian cattle browsed in the meadow above, the trees were in full glory, sunshine, spring flowers and the accompanying comfort of Benediction of unusual Catholic custom, thus Mary the vision became to many the reality it is already to the few. "Blessed Mary - Our Lady of the Park pray for us."

There was no feeling at all of being "traditional" no more yet antiquarian piety - the rapport and sincerity rekindled reconsecration and history was made on that sunny afternoon.

Father Timothy was assisted by Fr D St J Chadwick and Fr Ken Rogers.

Another report of the pilgrimage was written by Margaret Pollard in the Fraternity of Our Lady Bulletin no 57 dated August 1979.

Pilgrimage to Ladye Park
On 26th May 1979 Father Timothy van Carrapiett, with Father David Chadwick, led the first pilgrimage since the Reformation to the shrine of Our Lady in the Park at Liskeard. Some 50 pilgrims took part, members of the Guild of Our Lady of the Portal and of the Society of Mary. Br14 with his wife and daughters came all the way from Bournemouth. He was prominent in the first effort to win back the shrine for the church and it is thanks to his intervention with the Ministry of Transport that the present by-pass did not run right over the shrine and obliterate all trace of it.

Vespers of Our Lady were sung in Menheniot parish church, after which all proceeded to Ladye Park where a solemn procession was formed, a hymn composed for the pilgrimage was sung (send stamped addressed envelope if you want a copy), and with incense, candles and Holy water the site was "re-hallowed" and dedicated to Mary in the name of UNITY. History was made that day, though Fr Timothy's joy was marred because owing to the unavoidable absence of Fr Anthony Maggs, Master of the guild, he could not give him the Kiss of peace beside the well that was once the goddess Cerrid's Cauldron of Eternal Youth! However, he hopes for better fortune next year when perhaps an outdoor Mass may be thought of - possibly the beautiful poetic Mass of the Mother of Fair Love, the nearest equivalent of the Russian "Lady of Lovely Surprises", whose image, worked in tapestry, was carried in the procession by Br 154 framed in the fine velvet and gold border of an old church banner whose picture had disintegrated long ago - which had been retrieved by BR11 for our church, its title "Porta Coeli" making it very suitable. The day of the pilgrimage was the old feast of O.L.Queen of Apostles, the Saturday after the Ascension, and we hope it may prove possible to keep this day in future for our Ecumenical Pilgrimage.

Kerensa dre gesskrifa
Friendship through Correspondence

The next seven years carried on for Sister 13 very much as before, with her living a relatively carefree life, as a single person in London, but that experience she had had at Ladye Park was often recalled. She found herself becoming more involved in her faith and consequently more involved with activities in the wider community. Her family having moved from Truro she lost all connection with Cornwall until in 1987 she saw a photograph and article in the Sunday Times about Margaret Pollard and her Narnia tapestry which was in the Guinness Book of records that year. This coincided with Sister 13's sister Ann having been diagnosed with terminal cancer so she decided to write to Margaret Pollard to congratulate her on her feat of needlework and to ask for prayers for Ann. This was the start of a renewed friendship between Kate Pollard (her preferred name at the time) and Sister 13, which lasted until Kate's death in 1996. It started as one of Kate's many "letter friendships" and they corresponded weekly, exchanging jokes, quotations and views on everything under the sun. Kate introduced her to Vierzehnheiligen, the shrine of the fourteen saints in Bavaria, in her first letter, listing the 'specialities" of each saint.

"The fourteen Holy helpers are all very ancient, long forgotten Saints and all the more romantic for that. Here, briefly is the information;-
St Barbara; patron of the dying. beheaded in 307
St. Katherine: Patron of poor sinners and students. Beheaded in 307
St Margaret. Patron of women, specially in childbirth; beheaded in 307
St Giles: helps to make a good confession. Died 725
St. Denis. Helps with migraine; is shown carrying his head. Martyred in 119
St. Eustace, helps with throat diseases. Beheaded in 288
St. Blaise, Helps with throat diseases. beheaded in 288
St. Pantaleon. Patron of doctors and wasting diseases. Martyred in 302
St. Erasmus. Patron of widows and orphans and all diseases below the belt. Martyred 303
St. Achatius. helps in the hour of death. St. Guy (Vitus) Patron of youth. Put to death by torture in 303

St. Christopher. Helper against diabolical temptations and on journeys. beheaded in 251

St. Cyriac. Helps in very severe temptations and diabolical possession. Beheaded in 309

St. George. Helper at times of crisis of faith and soldiers in battle. martyred 303.

They tend to run in threes of a kind. Three virgins (Margaret, Katherine, Barbara), three soldiers (George, Achatius, Eustace), three bishops (Blaise, Erasmus, Denis), three laymen(Pantaleon, Christopher, Guy). Only one was not a martyr - Giles, hermit. There are also three dragons (Margaret's, Cyriac's, George's); and three animals, Eustace's stag, Giles's doe and Guy's Cockerel.

Kate then went on to try and persuade Sister 13 to go on the next Vierzehnheiligen pilgrimage saying they usually went at the time of the wine festival.

"Franconia is all wine country - you should have been with us at Volkach, there was this beautiful young judy with a golden crown and she had won first prize for the best vintage with her own wine and she gave us all a photograph signed by herself, and I got absolutely sloshed and was holding the Chief of Police by both hands and singing to him a German love song...they certainly got a new view of the English! Tell me if you know German and I will send you the fascinating booklet on the mysterious Staffelberg which is a small mountain with an ancient church and earthworks said to be Celtic - and a cave inhabited by gnomes called Querkele, like dumplings on feet. Your children will be fascinated. They'll all want to come!"

The children to whom she referred were the children whom Sister 13 taught as an infant teacher in an inner London school. As Kate was already in her late eighties, picturing the spectacle of her singing love songs to the Chief of Police seemed hilarious.

In other letters she wrote of her beliefs and ideas including;

DOUBLE DECALOGUE FOR A HAPPY LIFE

<u>*NEGATIVE*</u>
<u>*1. Avoid*</u> *interior heating (except a hot water bottle)*
2. Unnecessary washing, except not to become a public menace
3. Television
4. Self-pity, resentment and vain regret
5. Overdrawing your bank account
6. Medicines, pills and cosmetics
7. Amusements that cost money
8. The words "HURT", "IF ONLY" and "CAN YOU UNDERSTAND PEOPLE'
9. Meddling in what is not your business.
10. Letting your emotions be harrowed, unless it can result in immediate & effective action

<u>*POSITIVE*</u>

1. Continually count your blessings
2. Eat unlimited quantities of sugar
3. Answer all letters and pay all bills by return.
4. Limit your day to 12 hours and observe a strict routine.
5. Devote at least a third of it to prayer
6. Rely on black treacle and yoghourt for internal regularity.
7. Accept with enthusiasm all that you are offered.
8. Aim to amuse, gratify, edify or comfort people.
9. Listen with an air of being fairly hypnotised
10. Live each day as if it was your last. One day you'll be right.

Unfortunately within a year of the renewed friendship by correspondence, Kate's eyesight began to fail. The letters originally typed or written in her beautiful artistic handwriting changed to capital letters in felt tip on enormous sheets of paper as she struggled to see what she had written. Eventually she had to admit that she could not see anything she had written as her sight was "down to her eyelashes" but she never became down-hearted and continued to write even though sometimes she was not aware that her pen had run out or that she was writing lines and words on top of each other. She had memorised several books in their entirety and thousands of quotations before going blind and had instant recall, so as she herself said, she was never bored.

About this same time Margaret Pollard received a letter from Margaret Orchard a fellow Cornish Bard, president of the Old Cornish Society who had come across a copy of an account of the 1979 Ladye Park pilgrimage and had been intrigued especially as she had heard the house was now up for sale again The account was the one written by C H Jewell (Bardic name *Yuthe*l). Unable to follow her own advice on this occasion, to reply by return, Peggy sent a letter of apology in due course and at the same time enclosed some photos she had kept of the pilgrimage.

60 Richmond Hill
TRURO
Feb. 12th

Kersvarthes gar,

I could not answer your letter before for the simple reason I couldn't read it as my eyes are failing and unless a letter is written in bold capitals with a felt tipped pen or typed, someone has to read my letters to me and as there are double yellow lines outside my door no one can stay long so I had to wait till someone could. Howard Jewell's article is excellent and I am now sending you my photographs of the pilgrimage which you can have for your records.....the "Cornish Present" - "You can 'ave 'en, tidden no use to we."

It seems to be my life pattern, I am a bundle of straw that starts a fire and then I go out, and sometimes the fire is a big success and sometimes it goes out too, as Ladye Park did, but we were up against the Dark Powers and our guns were not heavy enough. You have a go and see what you can do. Naturally I regret that Our Lady could not win against the old goddess (ever read Robert Graves "The White Goddess") Swinburne would have understood. Cerridwen may be quite in sympathy with Bards and perhaps will be all in favour so long as it isn't the church.

See if the George's are still there. You will find them in the telephone directory. I bet it will stand long enough on the market and yet you never know, some millionaire Arab might snap it up and build a mosque... then there would be trouble, and I'd back the white goddess to run him out on his ear.

Dew re'th sowenno,
Arlodhes Ywerdhon (Margaret Pollard)

It had been mainly the premature terminal illness of her sister Ann, which had prompted Sr 13 to make contact again with Kate Pollard. As so often happens, it is at times of illness or disaster that one's mind turns to prayer and Sr 13 was in just such a position. Not only was her sister dying, but it was the period of the famous Cleveland case, when Social Services were very keen to take children away from their parents on a whiff of child abuse without discovering the true facts. Another of her sisters, Elizabeth, was battling in the High Court to keep her children from being taken into care or even adopted against their will. Ann seemed crucial in their plans to defeat the Social Workers, because she was to take out joint custody with Elizabeth, but now she was dying and the future looked bleak.

Many, many prayers and rosaries were offered up in the hope of a miraculous recovery for Ann, but within four months she was dead or as Margaret Pollard preferred to say, "She was promoted to Glory"

Right up until the moment Ann died, Sr 13, Kate, and many friends had been storming Heaven, invoking Our Lady and the 14 Holy Helpers of Vierzehnheiligen for help. When the prayers had seemingly gone unanswered, many mere mortals would have lost their faith in God and prayer but not Kate Pollard. As she immediately said, we all are born to die, and reaching the final destination for anyone in a state of Grace is a happy occasion. Any miracle healing is only temporary, but good, because it provides the lucky recipient more time to prepare and gives those who witness it a greater faith. It is the people left behind after death who suffer. She then went on to speak of times when large numbers die as in floods earthquakes, famines, epidemics and other so-called acts of God and said the good which came from them was much greater than most realise. From these events springs compassion. Humanity becomes aware of the power of God and the God within each person reaches out to the grief stricken and helpless. She said that without such catastrophes man would begin to believe he was all powerful and the weaker members would be even more downtrodden. Unfortunately it is only in adversity that the best comes out in us and we reach out to our fellow man. It is only in adversity we realise we need each other and ultimately need God and thus we begin to pray. She said that if only the world could change and recognise God in the good times, showing the same concern for fellow human beings and turning towards its Creator, she was sure there would be no need for such disasters.

Above: The beautiful Cornish coast
Below: Entrance to Ladye Park, before it was opened up.

Chaptra Naw

(Chapter nine)
An Bagas Ferguson ha'n Trest Gwlasek
The Ferguson Gang and the National Trust

By the time Dr Pollard reached the ripe age of 90, she was failing physically - she was blind and bedridden, but mentally she was still as alert as she had ever been with the same brilliant sense of humour. There was no sign of the wealth she had had in her earlier days. It had all been given to charitable causes. She lived in what some would have called squalor, but others an eccentric's paradise, in a small terraced former miner's cottage in Richmond Hill, Truro. She had moved there in the early 1960s when her Pydar Street home had been demolished for road widening. The tiny living room, into which she had somehow managed to squeeze a beloved organ, still had the original Cornish tin ceiling. The very basic kitchen had an earthen floor and everywhere there were books, papers and tapestries. Every inch of space was utilised including the walls, which were covered with her favourite quotations and sayings and for anyone whose first impression on entering was "What a mess", she had in bold letters the saying **"INCHES OF MUDDLE MAKE PATTERN IN YARDS (Me)** fixed on to one of the doors.

A few years earlier, when her age related disabilities had not yet taken complete hold, she wrote in one of her many letters that she was grateful for them rather than seeing them as a problem.

" *I rather tend to make the most of my arthritis to get out of all social engagements and lead the life of an anchoress which I like best - all the things I like doing best I do by myself, I hate travelling in a car or in fact travelling anywhere by any method, I find reading difficult now but I am reading, gradually, the "Ancren Riwle" which is a fascinating book. I always meant to get down to reading it one day and now Pat has lent it to me. These judies didn't have a bad time, they had their own houses and quite a staff of servants whom they could bully all they liked and if they grumbled about their low wages you reminded them that they were jolly lucky to be winning a heavenly crown by working for an Anchoress.... big deal! You mustn't keep an animal, but a cat, for if you kept a cow it might lead to mortal sin if the Hayward impounded it and you had a row with him and cursed him in violent language and you would have to pay up just the same to get the cow out of the pound. And he is absolutely obsessed with SIN especially SEX, he's really got a filthy mind and must have given the three judies for whom he wrote the book quite a lot of ideas. In fact in one place he thanks God they do not have the faintest idea what he is talking about!*

Like so many of her generation, Dr Pollard regarded use of the telephone as a luxury and only to be used for occasions of great importance. Nothing was more important to her than her daily tuning in to the Lord in prayer, so it is not surprising that the telephone played a part in this. Every morning at 6am for almost forty years she said the rosary over the phone with Brother 15 of the Guild of Our Lady of the Portal who lived in Camborne. For those unable to be quite so wide awake at that hour of the day she instituted a 7pm evening phone rosary for members of the Guild and it was said that in its hey day the phones in West Cornwall often became jammed as so many members were using them to pray with each other.

In 1995 realising that according to the law of averages it was unlikely that Kate would live many more years, Sister 13 decided the time had come for a trip back to her home town of Truro with the express purpose of calling on Kate Pollard in person. She travelled down with a companion, the intention being to combine the visit with a holiday. They found Kate in excellent form, delighted to see them, with an air of excitement about her. She was lying on her bed which was the antique chaise longue which had been in her previous home, now looking even more dilapidated. She spoke animatedly to the two of them, all the time showing her mastery of the art of conversation by balancing questions and answers and showing great interest in all they had to offer. At one point, explaining that her sight was non-existent, she asked if she could feel the face of Sister 13's companion so as to be able to visualise its features and match up the voice for future occasions. He was then asked the question posed to all new visitors to this amazing room,

"Which quotation from around the walls attracts you most?"

Taking a little time to peruse them in more depth he eventually decided upon:

"THE TROUBLES OF OUR PROUD AND ANGRY DUST
ARE FROM ETERNITY AND SHALL NOT FAIL.
BEAR THEM WE CAN, AND IF WE CAN WE MUST.
SHOULDER THE SKY, MY LAD, AND DRINK YOUR ALE"
A.E. Housman

Kate usually reckoned that she could read someone's personality or state of mind from the quotation they chose, but on this occasion she volunteered nothing.

"Now I have some news for you," she suddenly announced. "I believe Our Lady does want Ladye Park after all. It won't be in my time. I've always been like Moses, asked to start things and others bring them to fruition. I'm very happy to be used in this way but you are the chosen people. You will see the joyous restoration so, Sister 13 I'm handing the baton over to you."

Sister 13 did not know what to say. In the end she managed to stutter,

'But I don't even live in Cornwall any more. I have no money. I don't know anyone who has and I don't see how I can possibly do anything."

"You won't have to," was her swift reply. "Our Lady will do it all from now on. All you will need to do is to follow any instructions you are given."

Having always referred to anyone who believed they were

following instructions from "on high" as a bit cranky, Sister 13 did not relish the thought of getting involved in any such thing, but decided that it would be best to say nothing. Sensing her reluctance Kate suddenly added,

"I've one last card which I could hand Our Lady in case she wants to use it. I feel in my bones that everything has to be out of my hands now, but it's worth a try. Can one of you type a letter for me? My typewriter is over there."

She indicated towards an old portable typewriter lying on the table, almost covered with letters and other papers.

"I can," said Sister 13. She picked up the typewriter, noticing the lid was held on with a worn brown leather strap. Undoing this and removing the top, she inserted a piece of paper from the table into the carriage. The old fashioned two colour, red and black ribbon looked as though it had seen better days, so she typed a few words as a trial.

"As I guessed, " announced Sister 13, "This ribbon has had it. No-one will be able to read anything I type on this."

"Really?" queried Kate, "I'm sure it's not so long ago I used it. No-one told me they had received blank pages from me, but they might have done because I can't see a thing. Can you write the letter by hand instead then?"

As it happened Sister 13 had a portable word processor in the car outside, which she had brought down to deliver to her brother. She collected it to take the place of the defunct typewriter. While she was out of the room Kate turned to Sister 13's companion saying, "I think you should have a new name. How about Pegasus?"

"Sounds OK to me but what's the reason for it?"

Just at this point Sister 13 returned and setting up the word processor said,

"Fire away. I'm ready to begin. Who is it to?"

"I want it to the Editor of The Times Newspaper," she began in a businesslike manner. "I don't know the address but you'll find it on a copy of the paper in Truro Library. Then I want you to write the following:

Dear Sir,

On 1st February 1933 'The Times' featured the activities of a mysterious 'Ferguson Gang' founded in 1927. Its members went by the pseudonyms of 'Red Biddy', 'Bloody Bishop' 'Bill Stickers',' Sister Agatha' and 'See Mee Run'. No ordinary company was this, but one dedicated to curbing the spread of urbanisation and despoliation of the countryside by philanthropic means.

That gang was again recalled in the 1995 centenary souvenir brochure of the National Trust, mentioning that their identities still remained a mystery.

Though anonymity was an accepted law of the gang, times and circumstances change. By the time this letter reaches your paper one member of the gang will have been laid to rest in this world, though God willing he will continue his activities in the next!

By tradition bandits make a final request before they go *to their just reward and Bill Stickers lives and dies true to form.*

Having depleted all worldly goods in pursuit of Ferguson Gang activities, and others, he dies with one mission outstanding and therefore his final request is that the gang be opened to all National Trust members so that they may acquire Ladye Park in Liskeard Cornwall and preserve it for posterity. To this end he has appointed the first new member of the gang who goes by the pseudonym 'Pegasus'

My dying wish is (yes I confess to being Bill Stickers of Ferguson's gang) that Times readers be invited to send donations to the National Trust to start a fund for the purchase of this site of historical and religious significance. In pre Christian times it was a shrine to the pagan goddess Kerrid and includes her well of Eternal Youth. Later it became a place of Christian pilgrimage which though dissolved at the reformation still bears the marks of a place of beauty and peace

THIS LETTER IS TO BE HELD BY PEGASUS AND POSTED AFTER MY DEATH.

<u>Signed</u> *Bill Stickers*

117

Before Sister 13 or Pegasus could say anything Kate continued,

"Pegasus, will you go over to the bookcase and take out the book third row down, fourth in and tell me what it is."

Pegasus duly complied and read the title "England and the Octopus" by Clough William-Ellis"

"That's it" responded Kate matter of factly. "Open the first page and see what it says."

As he did so he saw on one side a hand drawn pen and ink sketch of England covered by an Octopus whose tentacles covered everywhere but Cornwall. On the facing page there was a hand-written dedication:

To Peggy Pollard
To whom
I would have
Dedicated
This Angry Little
Book
Had she been
Known to me
When I wrote it
Clough William-Ellis

"That book has meant a lot to me," she said," but now I'd like you to have it. Put this letter I have just written in it and only take it out to post after my death." She then took a £10 note from an envelope beside her bed and gave it to Sister 13 saying

"And I want you to put this into Premium Bonds for Our Lady. If a fund is started for the purchase of Ladye Park, cash them immediately to add to the fund. If they come up, try and use the gains for Ladye Park. Failing that buy some ice cream with it!"

Sister 13 was again rather non-plussed but she said, " I don't understand all this. Who is Bill Stickers and surely no-one is going to take any notice of a letter like this - certainly not the National Trust even if it got printed which is doubtful."

"You're right of course," replied Kate a trifle wistfully. "If the

National Trust did but know it they owe me a large favour, but no, that's not true, I didn't do it for them. They were the means to an end. The lot that are there now have completely different ideals so they wouldn't be interested anyway."

"Hang on!" cried Sister 13, "I don't know what you are talking about."

"No you wouldn't but I'm going to tell you two something now which hardly a soul in the world knows. It was quite exciting at the time but you must never divulge my true identity."

Kate then went on to explain how in her student days at Cambridge she had been very concerned for the environment and had formed a group known as "Ferguson's Gang" which anonymously gave large donations to the National Trust for various projects and how they had gained great publicity by getting their antics written up in The Times newspaper, which was very supportive. They were even mentioned on the radio several times. She then rifled through some magazines beside her bed, extricated one and said, "Does this say "Spring 1989?" It did and was a copy of *The Countryman* for that quarter.

"There's an article in here written about us. They still don't know who we are, of course, and never will, but the writer has been very thorough in his research and although there's a lot more to the story it'll give you a good idea of the background to the letter, but it's all so long ago I'd say the chances of it working are pretty low but you never know. If it doesn't come off, don't worry, Our Lady will have other plans. " Saying this she handed over the magazine open at page 50 entitled:

ON THE TRAIL OF FERGUSON'S GANG - Tony Oldfield

One of the more bizarre events in the history of the National Trust occurred nearly 60 years ago. The then secretary of the trust found himself the focus of attention by a mysterious group of masked individuals who invaded his office. All he knew was that collectively they were known as 'Ferguson's gang'.

I stumbled upon this story when visiting the eighteenth- or seventeenth-century Shalford water-mill, owned by The National Trust hard by the River Tillingbourne south of Guildford in Surrey. In the leaflet describing the mill there is reference to 'Ferguson's gang'. which anonymously raised the money to restore it in the 1930's.

Intrigued by this reference and moved by notions of relentless investigative journalism, I resolved to unmask the gang. So I first visited the National Trust offices and was given a file to read. A safe was opened and a dusty minute-book reverently produced. This was the minute book of the gang and would surely give clues to the identity of its mysterious members.

Not so; but much else of interest did appear. In the 1920's land-use planning was rudimentary. Sprawling development after the First World War, was increasing and many people felt great concern, One of these was the architect Clough William-Ellis, *who wrote a book about it* "England and the Octopus. " *This struck a chord with 'Ferguson' and a few friends. They had already formed a society dedicated to doing something to halt the sprawl.*

Members of the gang assumed names befitting a Dickensian thieves' kitchen and wrote letters in a fractured, low-life English. The founders appear to have been 'Ferguson', 'Sister Agatha', 'Kate O'Brien the Nark', 'Bill Stickers' and 'See Me run'.

They discovered that Shalford mill was in danger of demolition and resolved to restore it. The mill was generously given free by the owner. The first contribution of £100 in coins was made to a startled secretary of the trust by a masked woman in December 1930. Further payments were made in similar style. For instance in February 1933 'Red Biddy' delivered £100 in silver coins. The final payment was made with equal panache, on 3rd November 1933. It is not at all clear how the money was raised. Its formal discharge certificate shows that the gang had grown by the recruitment of such splendidly named people as 'Old Poll of Paddington' and 'Black Maria'.

Although the gang was formed in 1927, the minute-book shows the first formal recorded meeting was on 26th March 1932. By that time it had obtained permission from the Trust to use the mill for meetings. Although additional helpers were recruited, it was agreed that the gang proper should not exceed eight, because no more could be seated on the drum over the millstone.

Meetings always started with a vow to 'preservation of England and the destruction of the Octopus'. The chairman (Ferguson) would then ask; "When yew say England do yew mean England as represented by Whitehall or by Stonehenge?' to which the gang would ceremonially reply: "Stonehenge"!'

Other minutes contain charming resolutions, such as, after a day visiting a pleasant site, 'That this has been a lovely day', or 'That the gang may now go to sleep'

Some of this may be dismissed as childish play-acting, but it had an underlying useful effect. Long before the term 'public relations' became general, the gang knew what it meant. The minute-book has many press cuttings showing that the national press had become aware of the gang's existence and there were frequent references to its exploits. The anonymity and dramatic delivery made good press copy. This, of course, gave valuable publicity to the threat of uncontrolled development in general and to the work of the Trust in particular. The gang next turned its attention to the Georgian town hall in Newtown, Isle of Wight. This was derelict and was spotted by 'Bill Stickers'. It was purchased by the gang for £5 and an adjoining field for £100. Restoration was estimated to cost £1000, a lot of money in those days, and this was guaranteed by 'Black Maria'.

But the money was raised, with 'Kate O'Brien' delivering £500 in 1934 and another £500 presented later by 'Silent O'Moyle.' All these monies were delivered to the Trust's secretary in person.

In 1935 the National Trust was greatly concerned with the protection of the Cornish coast. Some land was already in its possession but an area near Sennen Cove was a vital piece of the jigsaw. The ownership of the property was uncertain. It was believed that it was owned before the First World War by an Austrian and had, in consequence, reverted to the Crown.

The Trust asked Ferguson's Gang if it could possibly raise the necessary sum of about £500. The request was made by writing to a

Mrs Peggy Pollard at an address in Cornwall. She appears occasionally in the files as the gang's 'front man'. She wrote back at first stating that there was some indecision in the gang; 'Ferguson' was away;' Bill Stickers' and the 'Bishop' were in favour; 'Red Biddy' was uncertain and 'Kate O'Brien' was against, but eventually she reported that they all agreed. Once more the money was raised and delivered.

In the same year, 1935, press and public interest in the gang was so great that 'Ferguson' was invited to make a radio appeal for the National Trust. Masked, but in a voice revealing that 'Ferguson' was a man, he made his appeal so effectively that, as a result, 600 people joined the Trust and £900 was contributed by listeners.

In 1936 the Great Western Railway had ambitions to extend its line along the south Cornish coast. Alerted to this, Ferguson's gang bought the land at Lansallos Cliff, east of Fowey, which effectively scuppered the scheme.

Then in 1938 their attention turned to Steventon Priory, then in Berkshire. some medieval cottages, associated with the Priory, came on the market and the gang once more picked up the challenge. It took two years to raise the money to complete this purchase, by which time the Second World War was in its grim progress. But the gang's pawky humour and dedication, in spite of those sad days, is well reflected in this extract from the very last letter in the file (August 1940) from ' Shot Biddy"

Ferguson have left I in charge and e don't want it said where he gone. This is the last batch what you are to get for them cottages at Steventon, see. I ope F. comes home soon I am a bit nervous of this job. They tried to bomb I last night but they hit a rabbit mister.'

From then on, silence. I have to say, therefore, that my relentless investigative journalism had been a failure and I have not unmasked Ferguson's gang which, in those pre-war years, had raised more that £4,500 for National Trust projects - a substantial sum at the time. However, after talking to various retired Trust Staff, I gather that, half a century after their heyday, at least three members of the gang are still alive. So - if you three read the Countryman *(and I am sure you do) - may we salute you who worked so hard at a*

critical time.
Reproduced with kind permission of The Countryman and the author.

Although Pegasus and Sister 13 only skimmed through the article at the time they soon realised the importance of the Ferguson Gang to the National Trust. Pegasus was himself a member and now vaguely remembered reading about it in some information he had been sent.

"Surely," he said, "your letter would hold more weight if you signed it with you own name instead of Bill Stickers. After all you are mentioned in the article so they know your connection.

"Never, never, never," came her prompt reply. "As far as they are concerned I was just a third party conveyor of messages. That is how it must stay for ever. No-one must ever know the true identities of the gang and you too must never divulge anything."

Pegasus promised he would not, and would never have broken that trust were it not for the fact that someone, he did not know who, placed a four line obituary in the Times on her death announcing that she had been Bill Stickers the leader of the 'Ferguson Gang'.

Maria Wynn a Gernow
Our Lady of Cornwall

Before leaving, Pegasus and Sister 13 asked Dr Pollard why she was so sure that Our Lady still wanted Ladye Park and if success was imminent. They asked whether she had had another vision. To this she replied that she had not had another vision or any direct message. It was more an inner knowledge which had come to her gradually, but which in the end had become just as strong as if she had been given a direct communication. In fact, she said, her conviction was even stronger than if she had had another vision for there was no doubting it. She confessed that her original conviction that Our Lady must win in the end had begun to wain, but a meeting with Philip Knight, a fellow Cornish Bard in early 1987, had restored it.

The story he later gave was that on his frequent shopping expeditions to Truro from Penzance with his family, he would walk down Richmond Hill from the railway station. He noticed religious notices and prayers in a shabby window. He was intrigued. Someone had told him that it was Peggy Pollard's home. As a Cornish speaker and fellow-bard, her fame as one of the early language revivalists had gone before her. At that time he had taught his eldest daughter, Suzie, then about 11, to speak Cornish and passing by one day, he thought it would be a good idea to knock on Peggy's door and introduce Suzie and himself to this venerable Cornish speaker. He was particularly keen to do so as he had taught Suzie the 'Hayl Marya' that he had found on a small woven carpet in the Lady Chapel of the Catholic Church in Truro, which he had later learned Peggy had made. She was most welcoming and listened to Suzie reciting the Hail Mary in Cornish. She spoke of walking the Sussex Downs conversing with A S D Smith (bardic name "Caradar" - lover of birds) a giant in terms of the Cornish language revival. He remembered her telling Suzie and him about Ladye Park, for the first time and how awe struck he was to learn that she had had a vision of Our Lady in Cornwall.

Peggy herself said that it was as she was relating the story again, the first time for some years, she seemed to go back in time to 1955. She thought of the many young people about Suzie's age she had taken to shrines of Our Lady around the world. She thought back to Our Lady's words and realised that time is only in this world and why should the restoration of Ladye Park not be in Suzie's generation instead of her own. She had only been asked to kindle the fires of its rebirth. That was the beginning of an idea, which became a stronger and stronger 'knowledge' until she announced her belief to Pegasus and Sister 13 in 1995 that they were among the 'chosen people' who would see the revival.

Philip Knight was not only a Cornish Bard and Cornish speaker, he was also a talented musician and songwriter and that first meeting of the two bards affected both of them in different ways. Every year a 'Pan Celtic song contest' is held to find the best song written and sung in a native Celtic Language. Philip Knight in

1991 won the contest with a song about Dolly Pentreath, the last Cornishwoman to speak only Cornish. The following year he wrote another Cornish song for the contest, which was the hymn entitled Maria Wynn a Gernow - Our Lady of Cornwall. In it the Blessed Virgin is asked to show herself in Cornwall, to watch over the land and protect it. . He thought, because of its religious nature it might not get very far in the contest, but it won the Cornish heats and Philip was chosen to represent Cornwall with it at the final in Galway. Peggy was delighted when she heard of its success in Cornwall and began to listen out for it on Radio Cornwall. Whenever she heard it played, which was quite frequently over the next few weeks, she sent up a barrage of prayers of thanks, together with petitions for its success in Ireland.

As this entry was more than just a song but almost a prayer Philip decided, after hearing Peggy's story, to go with his family and accompanist Mike on a mini- pilgrimage to Ladye Park to offer it to Our Lady and to pray for its success in Galway for the right motives and not personal kudos. None of the group had ever before visited the site, but they were not disappointed. They drove on Sunday 15th March 1992 to Ladye Park, which they found in its peaceful valley half a mile from Liskeard. Parking the car nearby they walked along the country lane, the first signs of Spring clearly to be seen in the hedgerow. As they passed on to its hallowed ground they passed through the small gate and over the bridge. Below it ran a shallow river, which flowed into a pond overgrown with rushes at the end of a large roughly mown lawn. On either side of the stream were the steep wooded slopes of the valley. These were once the haven of deer but sadly none remained, or if they did they were certainly not in evidence on this occasion. The ancient holy well could be clearly seen with its wild flowered covered steps leading down to the wooden door. With no guide they could only guess at the other remains such as the baptistery but nevertheless they all experienced a wonderful feeling of peace as they offered their brief prayers and then, after taking a few photographs, they returned the way they had come.

The International Pan Celtic festival is generally held the week after Easter and gathers Celts from all the Celtic countries - Ireland, Scotland, Wales, Isle of Man, Cornwall and Brittany. It celebrates old friendships and hereditary ties through their common bond of language, culture, song and sport. The aim of Pan Celtic, inaugurated in 1970, is to promote and strengthen Celtic languages and culture, whilst encouraging inter-Celtic tourism, trade, and commerce together with an exchange of ideas and information.

The festival is held in various towns and cities of Ireland. The first contest was in Killarney but both the 1991 contest (which Philip Knight won for Kernow (*Cornwall*)) and the 1992 contest which he was now entering with 'Maria Wynn a Gernow' were in Galway.

On Easter Monday 19th April 1992 Mike, Philip and his wife, Janet travelled by train to Galway - a gruelling journey - Penzance, Reading, Birmingham, Crewe, Holyhead. Thence they travelled by Sealink Ferry to Dun Laoghaire and then by a railway bus to Dublin station. After a wait of several hours by the River Liffy, they caught the Orange Train, which conveyed them across the somewhat flat, green pastureland of central Ireland to their destination. By this time it was late Tuesday and the contest was the next day.

They were not to win, but both Philip and Mike felt elated and proud as they lifted the engraved Galway cut glass bowl awarded to each nation's representatives. They felt they had taken news of Our Lady to Ireland, just as the early missionaries had taken news of Mary to Cornwall.

On the final day of the contest - a Sunday - there was an interceltic Mass in the magnificent Galway Cathedral, with its unusual Celtic design, and this incorporated all the Celtic languages.

The whole story of the meeting of the two bards, Peggy and Philip, was told to Pegasus and Sister 13 on the occasion of their 1995 visit to Peggy Pollard. Pegasus asked whether Dr Pollard had felt in anyway disillusioned that Cornwall's song had not won in the final after all the decades of the rosary and novenas, which had been said for its success.

"Not a bit," came her quick reply. " Prayer is never wasted! I always tell Our Blessed Lord to use any surplus prayers for any intention of his choosing. I look forward to getting to Heaven and finding out all the projects I've helped with. "

However she then went on to explain that she believed that Our Lady wanted that Cornish song and the Ladye Park hymn with the Cornish chorus to be used for some sort of Cornish Christian revival. She had no idea how it would come about, but Our Lady was full of "Lovely Surprises" and she just had the feeling that Our Lady had something special lined up for Cornwall. She then went on to talk about early Christianity in the county and particularly the involvement of Ladye Park. She asked Pegasus and Sister 13 in what language they thought the Mass would have been said by the very first Christians. They had not thought about that, assuming it had always been in Latin, but Peggy said she believed it must have been said in the local language used in Cornwall at the time.

"After all," she said, "the Cornish were great traders of tin long before Christ was born. It was they who introduced the Greek Ker to Cornwall and there were so many cargo boats constantly sailing to and fro the Mediterranean the Cornish would of course have learnt about Christianity from the merchants. There is even a legend that Christ himself came here during his hidden years with his uncle Joseph of Arimathea who was a tin trader. I think that very likely. In fact there is an old Holy well at St Minver called "Jesus Well" and people are said to have had all sorts of cures in the past as a result of bathing in its waters and reciting with faith the Litany of the Holy Name of Jesus three times. You can bet that if he did come as a boy, news would quickly spread back to Cornwall of what happened to him when he grew up. There would have been people here who remembered him. And even if that is just a legend, and he didn't come here, don't you see, Christianity would still have spread here very early from other Mediterranean travellers. There's another legend about Joseph of Arimathea that he went to Glastonbury, in Somerset, after the resurrection and founded the first church, St Mary's there. If he did come as a tin trader he would most likely have sailed at least some times into Fowey in Cornwall, which was the most busy tin trading port at the time. He wouldn't have travelled on his own. There would surely have been other travellers too, all anxious to tell their tales of 'Jesus of Nazareth' who they had met and some were no doubt fired with missionary zeal. Then there would have been others who had heard about Christianity second hand but still within living memory.

James and John were present at the Crucifixion, but tradition has it that James then travelled to Spain and converted nine Iberians to Christianity and was rewarded by the supreme gift of being visited at Zaragoza by the Virgin Mary, who was still living at the time. We know he had returned to the Holy Land by 44 AD and was martyred there, but if he was in Spain before that you can bet your bottom dollar that at least some of the Cornish traders would have heard of the goings on in Jerusalem - either via Spain, Greece or some other Mediterranean country and have been converted. It follows therefore that there could have been Christians in Cornwall even before the missionaries of the second and third centuries, most of whom came from Ireland. It stands to reason that if anyone was going to evangelise and persuade the Cornish to change from their native religions, and forget their beloved Kerrid they would obviously have to speak the local language.

If these missionaries were teaching the very basis of Christianity at the time, that the risen Christ was still present in the world through the re- enactment of the Last Supper or "the Mass" as it is now called, it would have been a fat lot of good trying to say the Mass in a language no-one knew. It would all have been mumbo jumbo and obviously the missionaries must have ordained local people to say Mass or else how could knowledge of it have spread. One individual missionary couldn't have been in many places at once. I'm positive they'd have all been saying it in Cornish. It wasn't until around the 4th century that Latin was made the official language of the Roman Church and even then you can bet that down here in Cornwall they didn't take much notice for generations even if they knew about it. After all there wasn't any post. How do you think any information got through to anywhere except very very slowly. No, I'd like to bet that Masses were said at Ladye Park in Cornish for a jolly long time. They certainly wouldn't have given up their beloved Kerrid for a God who didn't speak their language. Even when Latin was eventually introduced it is a known fact that it was only for the essential parts of the Mass and the locals understood these because so much mime was used. Just think of the Offertory and the Consecration. Why do you think there are all those exaggerated movements of holding up the bread and wine and washing hands? The words for these parts were the same every time so they would have eventually got to know and understand the Latin, but all their other prayers were in Cornish and this was endorsed by the bishops. Carew, Nance and other historians say the same thing. That is what the Prayer Book Rebellion was all about in 1549. The Cornish were being forced to use the Book of Common Prayer which was in English and they didn't understand it. They would much rather have continued as they were with their Cornish miracle plays and doing their own thing as far as Cornish went. I like to believe that in some places there was the occasional renegade who said the whole bang lot in Cornish on an occasion like a patronal feast.

What I'd love more than anything, now that the church has come full circle, and we have the Mass in the vernacular, is for someone to translate our modern Mass into Cornish. It would obviously have to be approved by the church but that wouldn't be too difficult. What would be more difficult would be to find a priest who could speak Cornish to say it, but with God all things are possible. I'd translate it myself if I were younger and could still see, but there are plenty of others for Our Lord to choose from and he will. Just you wait and see."

At this point Peggy began to get visibly excited. "I've just had an idea," she cried. "We've had the first pilgrimage to Ladye Park since the Reformation'. Wouldn't it be wonderful if we could have the first Cornish Mass ever, it would have to be in its modern form, of course, in Liskeard Catholic Church, followed by a procession to Ladye Park, with everyone walking down the Mass path singing hymns and carrying banners. Then we could end up with Benediction or some such celebration in the grounds of Ladye Park.

We could sing MARIA WYNN A GERNOW, or someone could, in Cornish. It would be wonderful! Perhaps someone will even write a new miracle play based on the rosary.

"Don't get too carried away." interrupted Sister 13 laughing," You have to admit you couldn't walk down the Mass Path now and it certainly isn't suitable for wheelchairs."

"That's true" said a not deflated Peggy, "If Our Lady wants it to happen, it will. If she doesn't – well, we can still dream and who knows? I'll see if I can exert some influence from the other side as I'm likely to be there before anything happens."

Above: The Bavarian village of Uzling
Below: Banner on the tenth station of the Cross

Chaptra Deg
(Chapter Ten)
An gober diwettha
The final Reward

Although very happy to remain in this world as long as possible, Dr Pollard knew that God could call her any time and she was always prepared for this. Nevertheless, she believed in using and living every day of her life to the full. As physical infirmity crept up upon her in old age, the subject of her moving to a nursing home was often mentioned. She refused emphatically, not because she could not bear to leave her home and her possessions; quite the contrary for she had worked on becoming attached to nothing, but she knew that, as soon as she entered a nursing home, all her pension would be taken from her. She only had the basic state pension and no capital, but to her this was a small fortune. Her own needs were practically non-existent. She used no heating, even in Winter, had no electrical equipment to go wrong, except a very old wireless, which was her constant companion, and her desire for food was minimal. Her personal living expenses were therefore very low, but she was supporting a host of "Roses" in Africa. This was the name she gave to the many black nuns with whom she corresponded, always including a £5 note in the envelope. The angels must have been on her side, because she said she always sent bank notes and never once was one lost en route. However, she realised that once she was admitted into a nursing home, all that would have to stop and as her roses often relied on her money as their only source of income, she wanted to last out as long as possible.

By early 1996, aged 92, Dr Pollard had to reluctantly agree that though her spirit wanted to stay in her own home, her frequent falls were becoming a worry for everyone around her, so she agreed to be moved to Kenwyn Nursing Home in Truro. Her house was sold and her possessions dispersed, but stoic as ever she accepted that this was what the Lord must want for her and she did not look back.

Kenwyn is a beautiful home and although bedridden she had more luxury there than she had ever had in her life. Mentally she was still as alert as ever, with even more time to spend on her favourite occupation, prayer. She had the phone connected by her bed and although the home insisted that she move her morning telephone rosary with Brother 15 from 6am to 7am, she continued with it until three days before she died, when she finally became too tired to lift the phone or speak.

During her time at Kenwyn she continued to have many visitors, some asking her to pray for them, some praying with her and some just visiting to enjoy the wonderful conversations on all subjects in which she continued to engage. Both Pegasus and Sister 13 were among the callers. Every time she would begin with, "Tell me, what's your news?" with genuine enthusiasm as though what they had to say was the most important thing in the world, but that was her way with everyone, always more interested in others than herself. She never once complained of any sort of physical pain, although she had bad arthritis so must have suffered some, but she doubtless offered it up as a form of sacrifice and at last on 13th November 1996 she was called at the age of 93 to her eternal reward.

In the month previous to Dr Pollard's death Sister 13 and Pegasus were planning their Christmas holiday for that year. Both felt they would like a 'real' Christmas with churches nestling in snow. They had seen Kate's photos of Vierzehnheiligen in the Winter. It looked a real wonderland, and so they decided that would be as good a place as any. They wrote off to the 'Pater Guardian' of the Basilica of the fourteen saints, asking for the times of Christmas services and suggestions for somewhere to stay. By return of post came a letter saying how pleased he was that they wanted to visit, but suggested that the Spring would be so much better, when all the wild flowers would be out and the walking magnificent. He said that at Christmas, apart from the church services, there would be very little to do. It did not take much to change the minds of Pegasus and Sister 13, so there and then they booked up for the following April.

Within days of booking their hotel, they heard the news of Dr Pollard's death and made plans to attend the Requiem Mass at Truro Catholic Church on Monday 18th November. The church was packed to capacity. Among the mourners were representatives of the numerous organisations and groups with which she had been connected. They came from all walks of life, of many religions and of none. They were indicative of her many and varied interests and accomplishments. The National Trust was not represented as at that time no one knew the enormous part she had played in its history.

After the Requiem Mass just a small band of close friends accompanied the coffin to the crematorium for a simple but very sincere final farewell and committal to the Lord. It was on the way back from this ceremony that mention was made to Sister 13 and Pegasus that Margaret Pollard had left a request that her ashes be taken to Vierzehnheiligen in Germany, her "Heaven on Earth", but no-one knew how this was going to be arranged. Pegasus and Sister 13 exchanged glances. They knew exactly who would be taking them.

A few days after the funeral, Pegasus posted 'The Times' letter referring to Ladye Park, which had been entrusted to him the previous year. He also sent a copy to the National Trust. Nothing came of either of these, but the National Trust had become aware for the first time of the true identity of "Ferguson" by means of a brief obituary notice in 'The Times' on the day of the funeral. It read:

POLLARD - Peggy (nee
 Gladstone) aged 93
peacefully 13th November
Leader of the Ferguson Gang
1920's. An outstanding brain.
Cremation Tregunnas Truro
18th November.

The secret of her involvement with the Ferguson Gang, which she said must never be divulged was out. No-one knows who inserted the brief notice. It did not mention the Requiem Mass nor the time of the cremation, but it paved the way for Pegasus (despite his promise) to speak openly about Bill Stickers in his efforts to make the bandit's last wishes come true.

During the following weeks and months fuller obituaries appeared in a wide variety of publications. It was impossible for any one account to give a full picture of the extent, to which her life touched others for the better or to list her achievements, but the account printed in *The Times Newspaper* and later in the *Plymouth Diocesan Catholic Directory* was more complete than others and was accompanied by a photograph. It was headed,

"Margaret Pollard, Sanskrit scholar and Bard of the Cornish Gorsedd died in Truro on 13th November aged 93. She was born on 1st March 1903"

The account was not signed but it was obviously written by someone who knew her well. It painted a picture of a character, "occasionally eccentric" of "intense intellectual and crusading activity".... "but fiercely rational and widely loved." It told of her passion for all things Cornish, how she learnt the language, studied the literature, involved herself in Bardic celebrations and acted as Cornish Secretary for the Council for the Preservation of Rural England for 14 years. Acknowledgement was given to her work for the National Trust, although (as to be expected) there were some discrepancies concerning Ferguson's Gang. Reference was made to her musical talents, including mention of a presumption that she wrote the ditty "Up on The Cliffs of Mayon Castle," which celebrates the National Trust's first holding (purchased with the aid of Ferguson's Gang) at Lands End. It related that that purchase included the rock known as the "Irish Lady" and allusions were made to the fact that she took the name "Arlodhes Ywerdon" when she became a bard at the Cornish Gorsedd in 1938 and was the Gorsedd harpist.

Margaret Pollard's strong Catholic faith was recognised and in particular her devotion to the Virgin Mary, which, together with her linguistic talents, led her to translate from Church Slavonic many akathist hymns, which are songs of praise to the Mother of God sung by the Eastern Orthodox Church. Even her re-establishment of the Guild of Our Lady of the Portal and her attraction to Vierzehnheiligen in Southern Germany were noted. There was only one strand of her life missing from the obituary, and that was her involvement with and interest in the Ancient Shrine of Our Lady of The Park. This had been kept private apart from the "chosen few", so when after her death interest began, like a phoenix rising from ashes, to develop and then snowball, it could not be suggested that this was as a result of loyalty to her memory. On the contrary, no more than a handful of people were still alive at her death, who would have connected any revival with Margaret Pollard, and yet revive it did!

The National Trust Magazine, somewhat belatedly, in July 1997, printed an article "Death of a bandit" and other accounts began to be written in all sorts of publications as news of Cornwall's loss began to filter through.

X a dhiskwa an tyller
X marks the spot.

The planned trip to Vierzehnheiligen in April by Pegasus and Sister 13 was originally intended as a sight-seeing and walking holiday. Now they had the unusual task of escorting Margaret Pollard's earthly remains, her ashes, to the spot. They were not sure whether they should call it a pilgrimage or an adventure. They decided it was going to be a combination of both, as that was how Margaret had always viewed pilgrimages.

Luck had it that around this time, a national newspaper was offering free travel on the newly opened Eurostar. Both Sister 13 and Pegasus collected the necessary coupons and duly sent off for their complimentary rail tickets, which would take them as far as Brussels. This seemed an excellent start and then the following weekend the same newspaper featured an advert for a special offer at the *Holiday Inn* at Koblenz, enabling them to break their journey at this beautiful city on both the outward and return journeys, with accommodation at a very reasonable price. They also availed themselves of this offer. They had already decided they would stay at the *Schwarzer Adler Gasthof* in End, Staffelstein, though they knew nothing about it except it was one of the few hotels in the area of Vierzehnheiligen. All that now remained was to organise travel from Brussels to Koblenz to Staffelstein. The German Tourist Board charged the earth for advice over the phone, so Pegasus decided to visit the listed address in person. It was extremely difficult to find, being situated in the basement of what seemed like a block of flats in Mayfair. When he did eventually manage to locate the building and to find his way to the actual office, he found himself in a modern brightly lit room, surrounded with posters. There were several friendly looking staff, but no other customers. The gentleman at the enquiry desk could not have been more helpful. He looked up the Schwarzer Adler Hotel and was even able to produce a brochure with details. He worked out all the train times, suggesting a change at Brussels and Cologne on the way to Koblenz - and produced a beautiful computer printout, which included the times of the train onward to Staffelstein the next day and to cap it all gave the price of a taxi from Staffelstein Railway station to the hotel. Leaving with several maps and brochures on the Main and Rhine Valley, Pegasus felt well pleased with his visit and was glad he had decided not to telephone.

With travel arrangements firmly in place, the next step was to plan exactly what they were going to do with the ashes once they reached Vierzehnheiligen. They felt it would be an anti-climax to travel all that way just to open a pot and let the wind blow some dust away. They felt that even just for themselves, there should be some sort of ceremony. They realised that their time in Germany covered the feast of St George, not only the patron saint of England but also one of the Fourteen Helpers in Times of Distress. This seemed an ideal day to commemorate someone, who had done so much for that very English organisation, the National Trust, with the added advantage that there would obviously be a very special celebratory Mass in the basilica on that day. So with this date in mind, they wrote off to the curator in charge of religious artefacts at

Vierzehnheiligen. Their plan was to attend the celebration in the basilica, then to visit the votive room where they had been told the banner made by Margaret Pollard was still hanging, if possible to borrow it, and then to walk in private procession carrying the banner to the spot where they decided to scatter the ashes. They realised that they would need permission to borrow the banner, which might not be granted to two unknowns from England, but they need not have worried. A letter in reply to their request came in no time. They had written in English as their German was almost non-existent. The reply was printed on beautiful official "Vierzehnheiligen" note paper featuring a design sketch of the basilica. The signature unfortunately was illegible, but the contents of the letter were delightful.

14 March 1997

Dear Pilgrims,

I have received your letter with great pleasure. I'll try to answer in your native language.

Have a good stay at Staffelstein for three days.

It is necessary to inform you, that it is not allowed in Germany to disperse a defunct.

but what you will do, that's your matter.

Naturally we rent to you the "Wallfahrtsbanner" in remembrance to Mrs Pollard.

On St George's Day there will be celebrated a Mass at 9a.m.

Yours sincerely,

Hoping that "rent" meant "lend" and not that they would have to pay some vast sum for the privilege and assuming that "dispersing a defunct" meant something other than what they had planned, they were very happy with this response and set off on their adventure a week after Easter 1997.

The journey went exactly as planned, with German Rail coming up trumps. All trains ran to time. Timetables showing platforms for each train were clearly displayed everywhere, making oral queries unnecessary. Ticket collectors were courteous and businesslike and, as soon as anyone realised they were from Britain, English was spoken almost automatically. Two days later, after one memorable evening in Koblenz, Pegasus and Sister 13 found themselves being driven the 6-8 miles from Staffelstein railway Station, by taxi to the tiny village of End, to the *Schwarzer Adler Gasthof.* As if someone had waved a wand, they found themselves in a different world. Neither the taxi driver nor anyone at the hotel, nor it would seem in the whole village, spoke a word of English but their welcome and friendliness was unmistakable. The village was still decorated for Easter with eggs all around the communal pump. The hotel they had chosen seemed to be the meeting point for every local in the vicinity and on that first night- a Monday - a wonderful local band played German dance music in the restaurant. From the moment the group first struck up until the end, the floor was packed with dancers of all ages. Many of the tunes were ones Pegasus and Sister 13 recognised such as "The Wanderer", but others just had that very distinctive German/Bavarian flavour.

With no-one speaking English, Pegasus and Sister 13 were amazed at how quickly one can pick up a language in case of necessity. Sister 13 had half-heartedly studied, via cassette, a BBC "Get by in German" for two weeks before travelling and had also brought a German phrase book plus a "German in Three Months." By the end of their stay, she felt it should have been renamed "German in Three Days" as they phoned for taxis, asked directions and even held some very interesting conversations with the other hotel guests.

The 23rd April 1997, St George's Day dawned bright and clear. A very early start was needed, for Vierzehnheiligen was 12 kilometres from End. Partly because there was no public transport and partly because they wanted to make the journey as much a pilgrimage as possible, Pegasus and Sister 13 had decided to travel to the basilica for the 9am Mass on this auspicious occasion on foot.

This was no hardship for both loved walking and the scenery was superb.

Planning the expedition the previous day they had stocked up on fresh fruit and rolls, knowing that the hotel staff would not be on duty in time for breakfast as early as they would need it. They knew they would miss the now almost standard tea and coffee making facilities available in English hotel rooms, but decided they would accept this as the 'penance' which Kate always said should be somewhere in a pilgrimage. In the event they made do with clear cool water from the local well which was hardly much of a penance. Dawn was just breaking as they set off.

The route took them over hill and dale, through fields and forest and past a beautiful little village called Uzling. It was obviously an official pilgrimage route as from time to time they passed wayside shrines dedicated to the Vierzehnheiligen saints. These were built of stone and erected in memory of someone who had died. The first one they passed was inscribed "Fischer November 1969 - November 1992" followed by a prayer. Fresh flowers adorned the stone as they did many of the other shrines en route. These all added to the atmosphere of pilgrimage. At one point Pegasus suggested that it would be fitting if a shrine could be erected for Margaret Pollard, but immediately he said it, he knew that she would have hated that to happen. Her whole life had been lived seeking anonymity. She would have been horrified at the thought of a stone engraved with her name, no matter which of her many names was chosen.

Almost three hours after setting out Pegasus stopped to consult the map. Just as he had expected they were a few metres above Vierzehnheiligen. They continued down the wooded path and suddenly as they turned the corner they saw Balthasar Neumann's imposing building rising in front of them, but this was nothing to what they saw as they entered via the small side door. Suddenly they saw the sun streaming through the window on to a sea of gold and rose-white marble in an enormous light and airy space where a throng the size of a football crowd would merely have been an irritation. In the centre of this elaborate Baroque church which "sets out to astound - and succeeds triumphantly" was the imposing Gnaden Altar surrounded by the magnificent statues of the 14 saints in very unsaintlike poses. St Margaret, Dr Pollard's namesake, was daintily swinging her golden shoe. It seemed fitting that she should be the first statue they recognised and all around were cherubs up to all sorts of antics and the whole atmosphere of the place was one of "fun". One angel was carefully wrapping someone's entrails around a staff. The owner had obviously been martyred by having them pulled out. Sister 13 could understand why Margaret Pollard had suggested the children would love this place, but afterwards neither she nor Pegasus could find words to explain what they saw and experienced on that first occasion. All they could say was they felt a tremendous feeling of joy, happiness and awe all rolled into one. Before this moment neither of them had ever been lovers of Baroque architecture, but now they understood why Margaret Pollard had called it her Heaven on earth and also why she said "Vierzehnheiligen proves that God is FUN."

The Mass was not due to commence for another 40 minutes, so the two found a spot within view of the enormous stage-set altar and quietly watched and waited. They had no doubt that Peggy Pollard's spirit was already in Heaven, but using her own precept that prayers for the dead are never wasted, being like spiritual gift vouchers which the recipients can use any way they wish, they prayed for her, they thanked God that they had this opportunity to be in such a wonderful place, they thanked God for the peace which now reigned between England and Germany and asked that it could spread all over the world. Then they prayed that the fire of interest in the Shrine of Our Lady of the Park, which had been rekindled by Margaret Pollard at the request of Our Lady could be allowed to burn brightly and be the means of a spiritual reawakening in Liskeard, Cornwall.

Lastly they pondered on Margaret Pollard's belief that some day there would be a link between Vierzehnheiligen, Truro and Liskeard. As they looked at the opulence surrounding them they could not think of anything less like the quiet, natural beauty of the Mass Path at Ladye Park and the surrounding countryside, but when they began to discuss this later they wondered whether Vierzehnheiligen could be paralleled with the Magi in the story of Christ's Nativity and Ladye Park with the shepherds. Christ came for everyone, rich and poor, believers and unbelievers, Jews and Gentiles. Maybe linking three such very different places of pilgrimage, Vierzehnheiligen, Truro and Liskeard would show that there is place in the church for everyone, whether their leanings be traditional or modern, simple and nature loving or representational. Maybe the three represent unity within diversity, so important in today's world. Truro with the Guild of Our Lady of the Portal and its international contacts could attract the Global enthusiasts, Ladye Park with its strong Cornish historical connections could become the centre for those wishing to include local cultures, from anywhere in the world, in their celebrations and Vierzehnheiligen could be the special pilgrimage destination of those who regard themselves as new Europeans. More important however, would be the fact that the same Mass would be said at each pilgrimage spot.

Gradually the vast basilica began to fill up with worshippers. The vast majority were men wearing medals or emblems on their lapels as though they belonged to some church organisation. Some came in carrying rolled up flags or banners but these were put to one side and not unfurled. There were no uniforms and no special places for anyone to sit and yet it was obvious that this was a congregation of a particular group of people. It was only afterwards that Pegasus remembered that St. George is the patron saint of soldiers and probably that explained the preponderance of men in the congregation. If soldiers are people who are willing to stand up and fight for their country, Margaret Pollard definitely belonged among them. She would have said that her armour and weapons were one and the same, the rosary, which she loved and prayed daily.

Next stop after the Mass was the memorabilia room where Margaret Pollard's banner was hanging amongst photos and souvenirs of past pilgrimages. There was none of the security so often needed nowadays in British churches. Sister 13 in her very newly acquired German explained to an official looking gentleman standing nearby, that they had permission to borrow it to take some photographs and that they were friends of the needle woman who had made it. Whether he was aware or not of the arrangements, they did not know, but he immediately took a long pole, hooked the banner down and gave it to them. No mention was made of when it should be returned, but Pegasus offered the information that they would return it within the hour, probably sooner.

They carried their prize possession showing the fourteen saints skilfully and amusingly worked together with their respective dragons or other idiosyncrasies. At the bottom in the centre was St Margaret holding a model of Truro Cathedral and they felt the deer portrayed could easily be from the royal hunting park at Liskeard. Making their way out of the basilica, they were intent on finding a suitable spot for Margaret Pollard's ashes to lie. Then as if led by some unseen guide, they found themselves walking the Way of the Cross, a most picturesque footpath with magnificent views over the valley and as far as the eye could see. The path wound its way round just below the basilica, which is situated on a hill and all along were stones featuring carvings of fourteen episodes in the story of Christ's last hours. The view from each "station" as the stones are called was breathtaking particularly at this time of year with Spring flowers dotted everywhere. Suddenly Pegasus stopped.

"This is where I believe she'd like her last bodily remains to rest," he declared.

They were standing immediately in front of the tenth Station of the Cross. "Jesus is stripped of his garments" The basilica could be clearly seen through the trees behind and the vast panorama lay in front of them.

"What could be better, 'X marks the spot,' where the earthly garments of Margaret Pollard, Dr Pollard, Mrs Pollard, Peggy, Meg, Kate, Bill Stickers, Sister 10, Mah, Arlodhes Ywerdhon, Cabhorse, and all the others, are finally stripped from her and she will be thrilled they are."

They hung the Vierzehnheiligen banner over the stone and taking out the small urn which he had been carrying all morning, Pegasus emptied some of the contents under two bushes, which were growing on either side of the stone and the rest he placed under a tree in front. Three spots were chosen representing the three persons in one God and the three shrines with which she had been so strongly connected, Truro, Liskeard and Vierzehnheiligen. A useful molehill provided soft earth to cover the ashes.

Conveniently a bench was situated immediately beside the stone. They were very pleased with this as it pin-pointed the position in aerial photographs, but also served as a wonderful 'pew' from which to say the rosary, the litany of the 14 saints and the words of the Vierzehnheiligen hymn, which she had translated many years before. Photographs were then taken of the pilgrimage banner hanging on the stone and under the tree as a record of this historical occasion.

Throughout this little *ad hoc* ceremony, Pegasus and Sister 13 had remained completely undisturbed, with no one else in sight. Then just as they were satisfied that all appropriate photos had been taken, an Italian couple walked towards them and offered to take a photo of the two of them beside the banner decorated station of the cross. How could they refuse? It was as though a photographer had been provided to ensure a record was made of the event for posterity.

Returning the tapestried "wallfahrtsbanner" they had one last action to complete. In the basilica petition book they wrote.

We thank God for the life of Margaret
Steuart Pollard/alias Bill Stickers, Kate,
 and many more, who believed
 Vierzehnheiligen to be the nearest
place to Heaven on earth.

God's great gift of life is ours
That we should enjoy it
And defy the infernal powers
Eager to destroy it.

Please pray for Margaret Pollard who translated the above hymn, made a "Wallfahrtsbanner" for Vierzehnheiligen and requested her earthly remains be brought back to her "Heaven on Earth." Her wish was fulfilled St George's Day 1997.

With all formalities complete, Sister 13 suggested that there was no way they could return home without guzzling one of the enormous German ice cream sundaes, whose praises Kate had sung so often. She had spoken of how on her last visit to Vierzenheiligen, her arthritis was too bad to enable her to join the other pilgrims on walks up the mysterious Staffelberg, or on any of the other visits to surrounding places of interest. Instead she had stayed all day interspersing "piety with gluttony", either sitting in the wonderful basilica, right where the sun streamed in through the windows and feeling bathed in the warmth of the light of God or shuffling up to the cafe for the largest ice-cream sundae imaginable and convincing herself that there would be no sin of gluttony in Heaven and as this was her Heaven on earth she could eat as many ice-cream sundaes as she wished.

It was not difficult for Pegasus and Sister 13 to track down the seller of these delicious creations and they felt not the slightest twinge of guilt as they spooned their way through the mountain of chocolate, cream, berries and ice-cream. On the contrary! They revelled in it, regarding this as yet another celebration of the life of an amazing person.

Having eaten their fill and taken one last look at the view from outside the basilica, the two set off on their return journey to the *Schwarzer Adler*. The outward journey, although most enjoyable had been marred slightly by their fear of getting lost and thus missing the 9am Mass, but there was nothing to detract from the beauty of the return journey. They took extravagant pleasure in the scenery, the sun and the many varieties of wild flowers, stopping whenever they felt inclined to rest or enjoy the view. At one spot they were spell bound by a sloping field, a mass of yellow and green. It was only on examining it closer that they discovered that the beautiful yellow highland flowers were none other than the humble dandelion. Never before had those Bible words, "Consider the lilies of the field, how they grow, they toil not neither do they spin........

Even Solomon in all his glory was not arrayed as one of these "(Matthew 6, 28-29) struck them so forcibly.

Next they moved into a shaded wood. Spring had hardly begun to show itself here. They walked along, enjoying a different type of creation, when suddenly they realised there was something strange about the wood. It was its stillness. There was not a bird to be heard. They sat on an upturned log to watch and listen. Absolute silence! No rustling in the undergrowth of unseen rodents, no squirrels darting from branch to branch as would be seen in England. It was almost eerie but not frightening. At last just two lone birds, too far away to recognise flew across the sky and that was all.

Sometime later they emerged again into the bright sunlight and the little village of Uzling they had passed through that morning lay before them. Its friendly looking houses were a welcome sight and even more so was a delightful village inn, where they sampled the local beer and had the equivalent of a delicious pub lunch, which at twelve marks for two seemed a gift.

Studying the map whilst eating, they decided to make a small detour for the last part of the journey. They could see that there was a marked route, which would bring them directly into the upper part of the village of End. This was exactly where their gasthof was situated, so on completion of their most enjoyable meal, they made their way to the centre of Uzling to get their bearings, but they had no problems in finding the route. That area of Germany is renowned for its walking and every footpath is clearly marked by a fine wooden signpost, showing the next main destination, followed by a number. At first they thought the number referred to the number of kilometres to the next destination, but when following the signpost marked End they found the number remained constant, even after walking for a good half hour, they suddenly realised that each walk must have a number to identify it, and indeed these numbers were marked on their own map. Sister 13 was a keen rambler back home and was astounded at how organised and easy walking was in Germany. She said she felt the English Tourist Board had a lot to learn from Germany on this score. Pegasus, with a Territorial Army background was slightly disparaging, saying he did not know what was wrong with carrying an Ordinance Survey map, but on the whole agreed with her.

Within what seemed no time, they found themselves descending a hillside path with the roofs of the houses of End in front of them. As they rounded the corner the decorated pump came into view and they realised their journey and pilgrimage for the day was over. They felt they had done Margaret Pollard proud and she had done them proud. It had been a successful and memorable day.

For the next few days before their return to England, the two continued to enjoy the wonderful countryside of the area as they tried out the many other walk routes, which were so clearly signposted from the village of End.

All too soon the day of departure arrived and after a taxi back to Staffelstein and the train to Koblenz, they found themselves back at the Holiday Inn wondering how to spend their final day in Germany. They felt they could not leave without a trip down the famous Rhine, but had been told they were rather expensive at £70 - £80 for a day of cruising. They had heard however that there were mini trips available for the equivalent of £12 for one hour and they decided to go for one of these. Someone however seemed to have other ideas for them and they had a sneaking suspicion that their friend "Kate" had something to do with it!

On arrival at the booking office they were told that the following day, the day for which they wished to book, was the 75th anniversary of boat trips down the Rhine and to celebrate this event the full trip entitled 'A Romantic Day on the River Rhine cruising between Koblenz and Rudesheim' would be the same price as it had been on the first cruise - 75 groschen, equal to £3.50 in today's English money. A traditional German lunch, including a bottle of wine and coffee was also 75 groschen, and so was coffee and kuchen. It did not take them a minute to decide to book up for their day of luxury cruising and that was exactly what it was. It was certainly a day which will rank amongst their most memorable, but throughout the day, whether they were viewing the famous Lorelei rock, or watching the waves gently lapping against the boat as they cruised through the wine areas of Assmannshausen, they could not but muse on the strange story behind the building of Vierzehnheiligen. Legend has it that in the 12th century a young boy tending his sheep reported seeing a baby in a field with a candle on either side of it. On reporting this to his mother, she boxed his ears and told him never to say such a thing again. She did not want the whole village saying she had a halfwit as a son. Inspite of this he reported the next day that he had seen not only the baby, but this time it was surrounded by 14 men and women, who said they were early Christian saints, known as Helpers in times of distress, who said they had come to ask that a church be built on this spot. They were reported as having ended by saying to him "You do a job for us and we'll do a job for you." The job he was to do was to arrange for the church to be built. There does not seem to be any record of what they did for him in view of their request having come to fruition with the building of a church. However, as Pegasus and Sister 13 relaxed on the sundeck in the gentle breeze while cruising through what seemed a fairy tale land of castles, including Heimburg castle with its imposing tower and the hilltop castle of Marksburg in Braubach, they could not but feel that this was Kate having her bit of 'fun' and saying. "You've done a job for me. Now I'm doing a job for you."

Above: The house as it was in 1990

Below: Detail from Liskeard mural, showing the Shrine

Chaptra Unnek

(Chapter Eleven)
Keweras Amkan a dhalleth
Mission begins

Once back in England, work and all the activities of everyday living soon began to fill Sister 13's time. However, she could not but from time to time reflect on the fact that Dr Pollard, who had so often said she was like Moses, starting things for others to continue, had died 40 years to the month after the date she believed she had been given the task to "bring the Virgin Mary back to Liskeard." Sister 13 also remembered words of Dr Pollard

"I pass the mission over to you. You are the chosen people."

She recalled that when she remonstrated her inability to do anything, Kate had said Our Lady would do it all. Nevertheless Sr 13 realised that any development would need humans to get it going, even if they were divinely inspired humans. She began to wonder how she would know if she was meant to do something. Unlike those who say "God told me to do so and so", Sister 13 had never experienced such knowledge and was sceptical of those who had. She felt she would need a thunderbolt, accompanied by an unmistakable voice from the Heavens, for her to recognise a message and probably would not even then, so she did not know how she would understand if she had a part to play. She felt, however, that she should make some sort of effort to achieve the desired end. Although the alleged request made by the Virgin Mary was

"Take me back to Liskeard", Dr Pollard had become convinced that this had referred to Ladye Park and that it was the old shrine there which was to be revived. Sister 13 felt therefore that this was where she must start. She knew that the Schneiders, the German/American couple who had purchased the house and site in 1978 still owned it. She also knew that Margaret Pollard had been in touch with them several times over the years and forwarded the historical details. Very good caretakers, who had recently become committed Christians, were looking after the house but Sister 13 had no idea how this knowledge could be used to bring about any progress. She had the Schneiders address, so decided to write to them on the off chance. She asked whether they had any plans to sell in the near future, and saying that if so she thought the Christian community might be interested. She added that she would be willing to act as an unpaid estate agent for these groups, but obviously not for the wider public. Almost by return of post came a reply saying they had tried to sell the property in 1990 but it had not been a good time. As they had had no success it had been taken off the market. They would like it to be sold, although they loved the spot, they now very rarely visited and when they did the whole time was taken up with arranging and authorising repairs and maintenance. Sister 13 was told that any expenses incurred for adverts would be reimbursed and the caretakers had been informed that they could expect prospective purchasers by appointment.

Suddenly Sister 13 realised she had let herself in for some work. There were details to be typed out, decisions to be made as to where to advertise, and whom to notify. It was rather a daunting task for someone, whose only experience of the property market had been buying her own London flat 20 years earlier, but just as she had found learning German easy when compelled, so acting as property agent was not so bad either. The information was circulated to various groups, who might be interested and adverts placed in well-known Christian papers.

The response was amazing. Each advert brought in on average of ten requests for information. One or two arranged to view and showed great interest, but none of these decided to purchase. Then in April 1998, Sister 13 found a message on her answerphone from someone, who lived in Hayle Cornwall. The message went,

"My name is Sheila Richards. You do not know me, but I had an experience this morning, which makes me very keen to visit Ladye Park. I am told you can arrange this. I'd be grateful if you could phone me back."

She did not know quite what to make of this message. The words had been to "visit Ladye Park" not "view" and she had an uneasy feeling, that this request was not in reply to any of the advertisements, she had been putting out, but nevertheless she returned the call and thus heard a strange story.

That morning, it seemed, the caller together with a house companion, Margaret, had visited a friend of theirs, Mike Jennings, who lived in St Ives. Among other things, he had mentioned his interest in a place called "Ladye Park". It turned out that this was the same Mike, who acted as accompanist to Philip Knight for his Cornish Song entry in Ireland and who had visited Ladye Park on a mini pilgrimage in 1992. The reason, that Ladye Park had come into the conversation that morning, was that Mike had received through the post a seller's information pack on the property, sent by Mr Barber of Truro, who knew of his interest and who thought he would want to know it was up for sale. Sheila had never heard of the place before and was not particularly interested, but as Mike began to speak excitedly about the site she found herself feeling distinctly unwell. She turned to Margaret with whom she was sharing transport and said, 'I think we'd better leave. I don't feel too well". "Nor do I" came the whispered reply so they both made their excuses and left.

Once in the car, they discovered they had both become very hot and then experienced a far away feeling whilst Mike was speaking of Ladye Park and were not able to take in what he was saying. It seemed an amazing coincidence that they should both have felt this at the same time. They decided that either they were both about to go down with some bug, or they were both allergic to something strange like a scent or chemical in Mike's house.

Starting the car they set off for their home, a delightful cottage surrounded by National Trust land near Hayle. The last part of the short journey was up the country lane leading to their secluded retreat. Hardly had Sheila turned into this lane than she pulled over to the side saying,

" I'll have to stop. I've got that feeling again."

No sooner had she turned off the ignition than she said she had what could only be described as an out of body experience and yet it was not out of body, as throughout the episode she knew exactly where she was. She saw in front of her a dark doorway in her mind's eye and then she felt something being drawn from her through the door and suddenly the doorway was full of light. She knew all the time where she was - in the car and certainly not dreaming - so she could only describe the part of her, which had entered the door as her soul and she felt her body had to follow. She had to find the door, visit and somehow turn the dark into light. Turning to Margaret to tell her of the experience, she found to her astonishment, that she had had a very similar experience, the only difference being that Margaret felt she was being called to go there and pray.

For both of them to feel unwell, at the same time, was strange, but not impossible, and yet for the two of them to proceed to have such a strange unreal experience was nothing less than weird. Talking through what had happened from the first feelings of strangeness to the awareness of the darkened door, they wondered whether the door they had seen could be the door of the place called Ladye Park, hence the phone call to Sister 13. Sheila in particular felt convinced that if she visited she would find that the door of Ladye Park and the one in her mystic experience would be one and the same.

Sister 13 listened to the story somewhat bemused. She did not feel it was within her remit to arrange a visit on these grounds and so she explained to Sheila, that her only connection with Ladye Park was as an unpaid agent and she could only arrange entrance to prospective purchasers. To this Sheila explained that there was a possibility that she would purchase the property, if she were meant to do so. She explained that she was fortunate enough to be in a position to purchase at the asking price if she sold her cottage. Sister 13 was still a little dubious, so like Pilate washing his hands, she gave her the caretakers' telephone number and suggested that she contact them direct.

That she thought would be the end of the matter, but a few days later Sheila Richards phoned again. She had made the required contact and arranged to visit the previous day. She recounted how as soon as she stepped on to the little bridge over the stream she felt Our Lady's presence as she had never felt it in her life. She was convinced this was a very special place. Before leaving home, she had put a film in her camera with the express purpose of taking as many photos as possible whilst at Ladye Park and she snapped her first there and then on the bridge. One of the caretakers welcomed her and showed her around the house and garden. Sheila continued to snap pictures through windows and around the garden, but when they came to the end of the tour she had a sense of disappointment. The 'door' she had seen during her mystic experience was none of the doors in the house and yet she had a very strong feeling that this was the place, to which she had been called. She turned to the caretaker, therefore, once more before leaving and said,

"I know this must sound strange but are there any other doors in the house or has the front door been changed in any way?"

"No" came the reply "but there is a blocked up door to the old chapel behind the bush over there."

Sheila walked over to the designated shrub and pulled back a branch. As she did so she gave an audible gasp. There in the wall at the front of the house was a bricked up door and it was identical to the door she had seen. She had no doubt about it in the slightest. The shape was the same and so was its position in the house. Her mind began to race. How could this be? She had never been here before - she did not even know of the house's existence until recently. She thought she was very happy in her country cottage, but did this mean she was meant to sell it and purchase Ladye Park in order to open up this door? She knew she had some serious thinking to do, so she thanked the caretaker who had taken her round and left.

It was the following day, that Sister 13 received her second phone call from Sheila, who explained the dilemma she was in. Sister 13 could not believe what she was hearing. Here was someone considering purchasing Ladye Park on what seemed to be nothing more than a whim. She began to question her further and discovered that she was a convinced Christian, of Anglican origin with Roman Catholic leanings, but not now attached to any particular church. She liked to describe herself as an ecumenical solitary. Having lived on her own for all her adult life, she had felt a year earlier that God was asking her to offer Margaret, a former Anglican nun from an enclosed order, a room in her home, where she could pray, surrounded by God's beautiful countryside, while she decided what she wanted to do with her future. The arrangement had worked well for both of them, slightly to their surprise, and that was still the situation. Sheila also spoke of how for several years she had assisted her god-father, Dr Kenneth McAll, a British surgeon/psychiatrist and author of a book "Healing the Family Tree" (First pub. Sheldon press. 1982,) in his healing ministry. This interested Sister 13 very much, because not only had she a copy of this same book, but had spoken to Kenneth McAll on the telephone a few years earlier concerning a problem in her own family. She had even arranged a "Healing of the Family Tree" Mass as a result of this phone call, so to speak to someone so closely connected with this internationally renowned doctor and healer meant a great deal to her.

The book, when it was first published, caused great controversy among the medical and clerical professions for in it Dr McAll tells how through his medical and religious experiences, particularly as a surgeon/missionary in China he discovered a remarkable method of healing many psychiatric illnesses through divine guidance. This did not mean that he did not believe that "*many emotional problems have their roots in a purely biochemical imbalance which requires medication, and this can be remedied easily enough when once identified, although it is not always easy to discover.*" (Healing the Family Tree) But he found that a number of patients sent to him admitted that they suffered from the presence of 'spirits' or the intrusion of 'voices', which were apparent and audible only to them and which psychiatrists dismissed as madness. However, he found this reminiscent of the traditional Chinese superstitions about good and evil spirits and he had gradually come to the conclusion that the spirits and voices were real and there was a distinction between them. Some seemed to be evil and often came as a result of occult practices, while others seemed to be harmless voices begging for help. He believed therefore that many patients suffering in this way and sometimes with other psychiatric illnesses were living their lives to a greater or lesser extent under the influence of someone else's spirit. The person, whose spirit it is, might be alive or dead, known to the patient or unknown, but for a healing to take place "*First, it is necessary to cut the known bond to the controlling person, alive or dead, then to forgive wholeheartedly, finally to transfer control to Jesus Christ, making any essential environmental changes to support these steps.*"(*Healing the Family Tree*)

When Sister 13 first read the book, she had felt very uneasy. It was not the sort of Christianity she was accustomed to, but as she had read on, it had all made sense and she had come to the conclusion that there was a distinct possibility that what he was saying was true and would certainly be worth a try especially in cases where all established medical practice had failed.

Sheila explained that working so closely with Kenneth McAll in his workshops, she had found herself aware, just as he was, when a spirit was calling out for help. This did not mean that she saw ghosts or had visions; it was just a strong awareness. She could have this feeling anywhere, sometimes in her own home or at workshops, but always in prayerful situations. She had seen many amazing healings as a result of prayer on these occasions. Then came the bombshell or it seemed like one to Sister 13. She said that whilst at Ladye Park the day before, she had felt very aware of Our Lady but also of many spirits in need of prayer. She felt that the light that was meant to be brought into the dark doorway was a light of joy for troubled souls. She believed that Ladye Park was to become a centre of prayer, where many people would find peace and joy in their own lives by praying for others and placing them in Our Lady's care.

She ended by saying that, having thought the situation over carefully the belief seemed to have come to her, there and then whilst she was on the phone, that she was not perhaps the one who should purchase Ladye Park, but she believed that very soon it would become some sort of Christian healing centre.

Sister 13 did not expect to hear from Sheila again, but a week or so later she received another phone call. Sheila had had the photos developed, which she had taken at Ladye Park and Our Lady had appeared in one of them! Well, this was very hard for Sister 13 to believe, so she asked if she could have a copy. To this Sheila hesitantly suggested that perhaps Our Lady had only appeared in the photo for Margaret and herself and that no-one else would be able to see it. This sounded the perfect cop-out to Sister 13, but she said she understood that possibility and would like to see the photo anyway. Sheila agreed to send it but explained that the photo had been taken through the living room window with a flash and that the flash had reflected on the window causing distortion in the picture and it was in this that Our Lady could be seen in front of the Ginkgo Tree. This did not bother Sister 13. It was on the lines of what she expected to hear as she did not believe that there was really likely to be a photo of Our Lady.

True to her word Sheila sent a copy of the photo the next day. At first glance Sister 13 saw nothing but a very bad photo - the sort one would normally throw away without a second glance, but having heard that Our Lady was meant to have appeared in it, she began to look more carefully. She saw absolutely nothing! Then suddenly she found herself staring fixedly at the centre of the picture. She could not see Our Lady or anything remotely like her, but what she could see was an unmistakable male figure dressed in medieval apparel. He wore a large hat with a feather. He had a dark beard and was wearing a short coat. She could not believe her eyes. Into her mind came the name 'Henry VIII'. This figure looked like representations of him in the film 'A Man for All Seasons'. It was in the exact position where she thought Our Lady was meant to be. How could anyone confuse the two? It was nothing like Our Lady. It could not be more like a man. She stared and stared into the photo, trying to work out how anyone could possibly see it differently, when suddenly she noticed another very distinct figure walking up the grass on the left. It was a monk wearing a long brown habit and he had shoulder length white hair. It was so clear, she could not understand why she had not seen it straight away. Then, as she turned back to the Henry VIII figure, she noticed another medieval figure directly behind him. He was a richly dressed man, with what looked like fur edging to his coat and a flat hat with a feather. Two other people not so clear were standing beside him. This was truly amazing. Sister 13 had asked for the picture of Our Lady, expecting to satisfy herself that it was a figment of the imagination and here she was, not seeing Our Lady but definitely seeing other figures. Who were they? What were they? Was she too seeing the bodies of spirits who wanted her to pray for them? No, that could not be right. Things like that didn't happen to her. She had not even been at Ladye Park, when this was taken, so how could the message be for her? Sheila had only mentioned Our Lady, whom Sister 13 could not see.

Knowing that Pegasus was about as down to earth as they come, she decided to swallow her own embarrassment at even suggesting such things and to show him the picture and see if he saw anything in it.

His immediate reaction was the same as her own had been in the first instance - a hopeless photo, which showed nothing except a white blob between two curtains where the flash had gone off. She then mentioned that Sheila could see Our Lady in the white light. He glanced at it again and said,

"Well I can't see anything. Can you?"

This was her opening, so she proceeded to show the figures she could see so clearly. If she expected to get confirmation of her own conviction, she was disappointed. Pegasus's reaction was that psychiatrists can see things in blobs of ink and fortune tellers in tea leaves, but as far as he was concerned this was just a very bad photo, which a flashbulb had made even worse.

"Surely," implored Sister 13 as she pointed "you can see Henry"

Half-heartedly Pegasus looked again.

"If I can see anything there I can see a soldier on horseback. Look, here's the horse's mane, here are his front legs and the soldier dressed in armour is bending forward."

"Don't mock" cried Sister 13. "I really can see the figures but I certainly can't see a soldier." She decided to put the photo away and say no more.

Over the next few days she showed the photo to a few friends, making it into a joke saying that a friend had sent it saying she could see Our Lady in it, but she herself could see Henry VIII. Could they see anything? To her awe at least 30% saw what she saw, when it was pointed out to them, one also saw a crucifix which then became clear to Sister 13, too, but she was very surprised when three separate people mentioned being able to see the soldier on horseback which Pegasus had mentioned. She had not been able to see it herself, so she had assumed he had been fabricating it in order to tease her. Now that others, with no foreknowledge of what he had said, were seeing it she began to wonder, although still having no perception of it herself.

She decided it was time to telephone Sheila Richards once more. Acknowledging with gratitude receipt of the photo, she said she could not see Our Lady in it, but that there did seem to be several other figures and wondered whether anyone else had noticed them. Sheila fetched her own copy and, over the phone, Sister 13 explained where the forms were. Sheila saw them immediately, even the knight on horseback, though she had not until that moment. She became very excited and said, "There must be hundreds of them there. We must pray that it becomes a place of prayer once more." Then she proceeded to guide Sister 13 to exactly where the figure of Our Lady had appeared. At that point Sister 13 saw what she was talking about quite clearly, but almost immediately afterwards it had gone and only great concentration could bring it back. The overriding shapes to her were always the Henry figure and the wealthy-looking man in his fur-trimmed coat as well as the monk walking at the side.

Pondering the strangeness of the photo later that night Sister 13 remembered an occasion when she had visited Ladye Park a few years earlier. Only the mother of one of the caretakers had been present and she had spoken of how beautiful and peaceful it was living and working at Ladye Park. She said there was even a ghost there. When questioned further about this, she had said there was nothing frightening or sinister about it. He seemed to be male and they felt his presence every so often. It was she said a very re-assuring presence and she liked him around. Sister 13 had thought she would not particularly want to share her working day with such a spirit-like creature, so when the caretaker returned, she asked her about this story. There was a laugh in reply and the admonition, "I'm afraid my mother has a very vivid imagination. She has only just come here, but we've been here for years. We have children and animals and I can satisfy you that no one has seen or heard anything except the beautiful birds in the trees and the occasional squirrel. They say animals are the first to sense anything abnormal and I assure you ours are very happy and contented. Sorry to disappoint you."

Sister 13 had thought no more about the episode, but now as she tried to rationalise her thoughts concerning the photo, she could not help but think back to that incident. She believed at the time it had just been a case of vivid imagination, so perhaps as Pegasus had suggested, her interpretation of the photo now was also just graphic fancy.

Whether or not the intruders into Sheila Richards' photo were real or imaginary, Sister 13 did not know but it marked the beginning of a series of happenings, which convinced her of one thing. When Kate had said that any revival in Liskeard would be of Our Lady's own doing and that there would be no need for anyone personally to feel they had to do anything, she was correct.

At the beginning of May 1998, about a month after Sheila Richards had visited Ladye Park, Sister 13 received another phone call. This time it was from Michael Jennings who said he was secretary of the Cornish Branch of the Ecumenical Society of the Blessed Virgin Mary (ESBVM). He thought she might be interested that they had arranged a pilgrimage to Ladye Park in the month of July. Sister 13 most certainly was interested. She had heard nothing about it previously and did not at the time realise that the caller was none other than the Mike, who Kate Pollard had mentioned as the accompanist, when Philip Knight had taken his "MARIA WYNN A GERNOW" song to the Pan Celtic Contest in

Ireland in 1992. He was also the person, at whose house Sheila had been, when she had first heard of Ladye Park. This seemed an amazing step forward! Sister 13 thought she had been the only one battling away to fulfil Kate's mission, but it looked as though Our Lady really was doing her bit and getting things moving. She was thrilled, when she heard that the date chosen for the pilgrimage was to be Saturday 11th July. This was the feast of St Benedict. Newspaper articles printed after the event spoke of how apt the choice of day had been, bearing in mind the fact that there were once Benedictine hermits dwelling at Ladye Park, but Mike was quick with an assurance, that he had no idea of the significance when he made the arrangements and what is more he felt sure it was only an assumption, that the hermits would have been Benedictines. He had never come across any records, which stated this.

The pilgrimage day dawned cold and wet. Sister 13 had travelled from London the previous day with Keigwyn Trenerry a colleague who also hailed from Cornwall, but who had hardly returned over the past 20 years. She had heard a great deal about Ladye Park from Sister 13 and wanted to see it for herself. On arrival in Liskeard they had visited "Grandma's Pantry" in Pig Meadow Lane for a traditional Cornish cream tea. They had noticed a mural on the wall, but there were cars in front of it, so they did not bother to investigate further. The following day they hurried through the lane again, this time sheltering under umbrellas and intent on reaching their destination in the car park. They had arranged to meet some other pilgrims there, to walk with them down the Mass Path before the pilgrimage. They were late, so looked to neither left nor right as they passed the mural.

For Sister 13 the pilgrimage was a very emotional experience. It seemed very strange, that within two years of Dr Pollard's death such an event should be organised, seemingly with no link to the previous one 19 years earlier. Sister 13 wondered whether she would have the *"omglywans na yllir y styrya"* (inexplicable feeling), which she had experienced on that occasion. She did not, but the event is best described in the words of Philip Knight, whose account was published in the Plymouth Diocesan Directory for 1999.

****

Ecumenical devotion to our Ladye of Cornwall manifests itself at Ladye Park Liskeard
by Philip Knight

On Saturday, 11th July, a group of some 54 Roman Catholic and Anglican pilgrims made their way to a tranquil and little frequented location. They were members and guests of the Cornish branch of the Ecumenical Society of the Blessed Virgin Mary. Some had travelled from London while others had gathered from all over Cornwall, both clergy and laity, to proceed from the rendezvous down the lane bordered by lush and verdant plant life on the approach to their destination, raincoats and umbrellas at the ready.

Nestling in the most peaceful of vales, a stones throw from Liskeard, is Ladye Park. Today it consists of a farmhouse and its grounds. To pass on to its hallowed ground, one-steps through the gate and over a bridge, below which runs a small river, feeding a marshy pond at the end of a large grassy sward, before journeying on down the valley. On either side of the stream are the steep wooded slopes of a valley, once the haven of deer.

The farmhouse itself, at present a home in private hands with caretaker-residents, bears relics of a far older building some of whose masonry - an arch, a mullion and a number of worked stones for example - forms part of the fabric of the newer structure which, nevertheless, has a room known as "The Monks Room". In fact hidden beneath a canopy over laurel foliage to the left of the imposing farmhouse, an almost complete end wall of an ancient chapel, once the focus of pilgrimages at least as far back as the 14th century, leans, clad with moss against a bank of earth. One fervent pilgrim placed a cross, fashioned from two twigs, in a square niche in the wall, and a beautiful statue of Our Lady was placed temporarily where the Holy Altar must have been. And just a few yards away, a short curling set of steps leads down to a well, almost certainly an integral feature of the chapel originally, when it would have been enclosed in a finely carved well-house. (Today it was covered with a profusion of wild flowers). Later, the water was to supply the farm, yet in pre-Christian times the spring may well have been in use when devotion to a Celtic goddess gave the *Liskeard its name (Lys Kerrid=Court of Cerrid)*.

For on this site was a shrine dedicated to Our Blessed Lady. Records show that there stood here, as early as 1310, a chantry, a 'celebrated pilgrim chapel' served by a series of a hermits, with royal permission to collect alms throughout the realm. Here, one prayed for the souls of those alive or dead, or paid for Masses to be said so that indulgences might be granted. Hence a small grassy path which has its exit almost opposite the entrance to Ladye Park is to this day known as 'The Mass Path'.

By the entrance, there was formerly a Baptistery conveniently situated where the bridge is today, in the stonework of which a hollow may be seen where one may less than fancifully imagine a statue of Our Lady to have stood overlooking those to be baptised, until suppression at the time of the Reformation caused its removal.

On this unifying occasion however, we were more than adequately immersed by a heavens that opened! The procession made its way down the lane leading to Ladye Park to strains of Marian hymns, decades of the rosary and with the society banner held aloft, and likewise a purpose-built tapestry, the pilgrimage banner portraying "Our Ladye of the Park ", woven by Dr Margaret Pollard many years earlier. Undaunted by the copious rain, the pilgrims were afforded a measure of shelter by the 'vault' of laurel foliage, where a hymn to 'Our Ladye of the Park', the words of which were specially written by Dr Margaret Pollard some 20 years ago, was fervently rendered to the tune of 'Daily Daily Sing to Mary'. After a 'Jubilee Prayer' seeking God's blessing in the Second Millennium, the 'Hayl Maria' in Cornish and prayers for 'Christian Unity' pilgrims strolled the grounds, a perfect setting for peaceful meditation, albeit under a more than moist Sky; and, having inspected those hallowed surroundings, the pilgrims returned to the coach suitably rounding off their day with a visit to one of Cornwall's old and beautiful churches, that of St. Pratt and St.

Hyacynth in the idyllic village of Blisland, where several images of the Blessed Virgin suggested to them the extent of her influence in Cornwall.

Indeed, at this point something needs to be said of 'Peggy' Pollard at whose instigation an attempt to revive the veneration of the shrine took place 19 years ago on the last Saturday of Mary's month of May in 1979 in the same setting though under vastly different weather conditions. Audrey Cawley, up from London, recalled as one of Peggy's catechetical group at Truro, her great intellect and enormous spirituality. Audrey recalled how Peggy had recounted to her (as to me later on 1st May, 1992) how, at 9 p.m. on 2nd November, 1955, when living in Pydar Street in Truro, she was aware of a blue light, and found a person, dressed in blue, sitting opposite her in an armchair. Naturally enough, Peggy sought to identify, and was addressed in Russian (Peggy told me she could say the rosary in 10 languages!). Apparently, it was Our Lady who spoke to her saying, 'You've been a good cab-horse for me, but now I want a ride myself. Lanherne is not enough for Cornwall. I want to come back to Liskeard!' A lucid and dubious Peggy (who had once written an irreverent skit of a miracle play in Cornish earlier, when her convictions had been less certain!) questioned the validity of her vision since, as she reasoned, people have 'visions' every day. She requested that Our Lady, if it were she, permit her to make a sketch (on a nearby envelope, as it so happened!) on which she might later base a painting. She would then send this to the Paris Salon. If they accepted it, as was, later the case, then she would read this as a sign that she had indeed received a special vision.

Peggy followed this up later only to find plentiful evidence at the Cornish Record Office, for example, that there did in fact exist a site of a chantry and shrine in honour of Our Lady in Liskeard, called Ladye Park. Consequently, she examined ways of regenerating the devotion there in accordance, as it seemed, with Our Lady's wishes. The result was the ecumenical service held there on 29th May, 1979. However, as Peggy says in a letter, "it seems to be my life's pattern, I am a bundle of straw that starts a fire and then I go out, and sometimes the fire is a big success and sometimes it goes out too, as Lady Park did........"

The loss of Dr Margaret Pollard to the world on November 13th, 1996 (aged 93), might indeed have spelled the return of Lady Park to obscurity, yet such was its effect and hers on those introduced to them both that now the torch has been borne in hand by others, particularly the Ecumenical Society of the Blessed Virgin Mary. Next year, it is hoped to mark the momentous 20th anniversary of Peggy's revival of pilgrimages to Ladye Park in grander fashion. Now, as it comes to light that Ladye Park is up for sale, what better than to promote Christian Unity by a joint venture on the part of our Christian churches in Cornwall. Perhaps the water of life might be complemented by the fire of the Holy Spirit and 'Our Lady of The Park' become once more "Cornwall's Dowry!"

Lymnans-fos yn bownder Pras an Hoghes
Pig Meadow Lane Mural

Soaked through but elated after the uplifting experience of the pilgrimage, Keigwyn and Sister 13 chose to return up the Mass Path to the centre of Liskeard for another visit to "Grandma's Pantry" for a warming cup of tea. As they returned to Pig Meadow Lane again, Keigwyn remarked on the mural, now unobstructed by parked cars.

"That's an impressive work of art. When was it painted?"

"I've no idea. I noticed it yesterday, but can't say I have before," replied Sister 13.

"It looks like the history of Liskeard" said Keigwyn. "I wonder whether Ladye Park is on it "

"Very unlikely" responded Sister 13 walking towards it. "Hardly anyone knows of its existence." But even as she was walking Sister 13 had a conviction that she would see it there. And she did. The mural is 44 ft long, 12 ft high in places, with an imposing 9 ft statue of Caradoc as the centre piece, but the two walked straight to the left hand corner. Sister 13's heart missed a beat. How could this be? A beautiful painting of the Virgin Mary, holding a white rose, stood in the opening of a Cornish roundhouse with a cross on the top.

Around the doorway were the words "Our Lady in the Park". At the base to the left were blue and pink flowers and to the right the tree of knowledge. From the forest behind leapt Herne the Hunter, indicating the artist was also aware of its pre-Christian connections. At the time Sister 13 thought this was one of the royal deer. Still further behind was a Celtic cross, just below the portrayal of the rolling Cornish hills. One hill was particularly familiar and she felt sure it must be Caradon, a local beauty spot famous for its archaeological remains. Only a few weeks earlier she had been at Minions, high up on Bodmin Moor, overlooking those hills in reality, meditating on a poem by Robert Stephen Hawker - Hawker of Morwenstow. She had found it in his book "Cornish Ballads and Other Poems" annotated and last published in 1908

****

A Rapture on the Cornish Hills
By Robert Stephen Hawker

I stood at the foot of Rocky Caradon -
The massive monuments of a vast religion,
Piled by the strength of unknown hands, were there
The everlasting hills, around, afar,
Uplifted their huge fronts, the natural altars
Reared by the Earth to its surrounding God.
I heard a Voice, as the sound of many waters:-
"What do'st thou here, Man that is born of woman?
The clouds may haunt these mountains; the fierce storm
Coiled in his caverned lair - that wild torrent
Leaps from a native land; but Man! O Lord!
What doth **he** here!"
Stranger.
Did'st thou not fear the Voice?
The Bard
I could not, at the foot of Rocky Caradon

****

She had found the note printed at the bottom of the page as fascinating as the poem itself:

Note
There is a wide extent of hilly moorland stretching from Rough Tor to Caradon and heaped with rude structures of various kinds, that would reward the researchers of an Antiquary. The cromlech, piled rocks, and unhewn pillars, are commonly referred to the times of Druidical worship. To me, they seem to claim a more ancient origin. A simple structure of stone was the usual altar and monument of the Patriarchal religion. The same feelings would actuate the heirs of that creed in Cornwall as in Palestine; and the same motives would induce them to rear a pillar there, and to pour oil thereon, and to call it the Place of GOD
(From Records of the Western Shore, 1832, excluded from Mr Godwin's collection.)

Awed and silent, Sister 13 and Keigwyn viewed the rest of the mural featuring tin mining, the Civil war, the town's castle, its charters, two tents to depict the towns markets, St Martin's parish church, the railway viaduct, the train which ran up to the Cheesewring around 1840, the library, Stuart House, the war memorial and the people of the town from the turn of the century and the youth of today. It was at this point they noticed another astounding feature. In the far right was painted a teenager wearing a sweatshirt featuring an oval emblem, the centre of which was a dove. At the base of the emblem was H.O.P.E.2000 in bold lettering. The year was still 1998, so this they decided must be a Millennium mural. How wonderful to have one featuring the shrine of Our Lady of the Park at one end and the Holy Spirit at the other. Did it mean that in the new millennium the Holy Spirit would become present in Liskeard in some tangible way?

"This is pretty powerful stuff" said Keigwyn at last. Who is the mural painter?

They looked at the stone engraved: DAVID WHITTLEY 1998

"I'm going to ring the local council on Monday to find out more about this mural" stated Sister 13 - and so Monday morning found her on the phone to the town hall. At first she asked if anyone could give her details of the Millennium Mural, but she was told that there was no such thing. A suggestion was made that she contact the chairman of the mural committee, so that was the next call. Even he did not know, what she was talking about when she spoke of the Millennium mural, but when he heard she was referring to the one in Pig Meadow Lane he laughed and said, "That's nothing to do with the millennium. It is just something to brighten up Liskeard" Unconvinced, Sister 13 felt she wanted to contact the artist David Whittley himself and asked whether the chairman would be willing to pass on a letter to him. His response was that he thought he would be delighted to hear from her and so he passed on the address and phone number.

That evening she telephoned David, who was fascinated to hear that there were still remains of the ancient shrine in existence. He had no idea and had featured it in the mural merely as a result of a couple of lines in a very old book he had found in the library, mentioning a ruined pilgrim chapel, which had once been a famous shrine to Our Lady in the Park. On the spur of the moment, Sister 13 asked him whether he painted commissions and if so whether he could paint her a picture of Our Lady based on the portrayal in his mural. He admitted he did and would get some ideas together and then speak to her about them before beginning anything. In return, she promised to send him some of the details she had been given by Dr Pollard of the old shrine.

At the Saturday pilgrimage, inspite of the pouring rain, Keigwyn had tried to take some photographs. She did not expect them to come out very well, but took them into Boots in Liskeard to get them developed before their return home. On calling to collect them on the Tuesday morning, she opened them in the store to have a quick peep. The first picture was of a baby, which she could not quite understand, but then she realised that all the photographs were of the same baby. She realised immediately that there must have been some mix up and the true owner of the baby pictures must have her Ladye Park ones. She immediately returned them, thinking it would be quite easy to trace hers, but it seemed this was not the case, because all photos from all stores are sent to a central depot for developing and therefore her photos could have been sent to any branch of Boots in the South West. It would be a case of someone else reporting they had the wrong photos, returning them to the store from where they had collected them. The store in turn would have to return them to the depot, where they had descriptions of missing photographs. It seemed a very long process and there was obviously no chance of Keigwyn's being found before the return home, so she left her address and hoped and prayed. Two weeks later the photos arrived safely in the post.

This annoyance would not normally be worth recording, but in the light of the strange occurrences concerning photographs before and after this event it is perhaps worth mentioning.

A week or so after returning, Sister 13 posted to David Whittley the promised notes on the history of the shrine of Our Lady in the Park, including details of where it was, as he had said he had no idea where the site had been. He had hinted during their phone call that there had been incidents connected with the painting of the mural which were quite puzzling. This had raised Sister 13's curiosity, so she asked if he could supply any details. On 28th July she received a most welcome reply.

David Whittley
SALTASH
Cornwall
PL124EY
26/7/98

Thank you very much for all the information on Ladye Park. It was lovely to talk to you on the telephone and to receive your letter. Where do I start; there are certainly a lot of coincidences regarding the mural and the chapel of Our Lady in the Park. I think something very positive is taking place. Firstly the mural has had a brilliant response from the locals, from tiny tots to senior citizens, all have responded with interest and curiosity, which seems to have awakened a feeling of awareness and belonging, identifying with various aspects of the mural theme, which is great because I see the mural as part of the community.

As said before I had no idea of the history of Liskeard when first setting out on this project. I am not Cornish, originating in Norfolk. To give a brief outline of my background: Left school at fifteen. My family have a background of fishers and trawler men. I joined the merchant navy. After a few years of travelling I joined the Royal Marine Commando's in 1965. Leaving the marines in the early seventies, became a commercial driver. Eventually I took on the role of builder. It is only in the last two years that I have been a professional artist, although I have painted for many years prior. So I have no "training"

The way I paint is by feel rather than right (hope that does not sound silly!) and this is especially true of the mural. For instance, having no preconceived idea of how I might present the chapel of Our Lady in the Park, I spent several nights just emptying my mind and seeing what came into it. Sometimes I got little glimpses of bits, other times the whole thing explodes into view very strongly, easy enough to remember. Originally the chapel in my plan was empty - with maybe the cross being barely visible. Two days before I actually painted it on the wall, the sight of the Virgin clutching a small white rose came into my mind and would not go away, so I painted it the way it wanted to be, it felt very right to me.

Strangely enough there have been other 'little things' about the mural. When first painting Caradoc, on the second day, a group of rowdy young lads came along. One of the boys stopped in his tracks and actually shouted out to his friends, "It's him, its him in my dream."

The boy asked me who he was and then explained that about a month before, he had a recurring dream. Caradoc was on the wall as he is, the boy and his friends were throwing stones and bottles at him, then Caradoc became alive and chased the boy, frightening him severely! He then said to me, "I'll never do anything to this mural", thanked me and went off with his mates. I think he was very serious. (I have looked on Caradoc as a kind of guardian of the mural. That's why he stares at you wherever you are. I designed him that way!)

The second incident was a few days later. Two elderly ladies came over to me and asked who the giant figure was. When I replied "Caradoc, but of course I have had to imagine what he might have looked like." They both said together, "Oh yes, that's Caradoc alright!" and walked away grinning, without saying any more. I have never seen them since, unlike a lot of locals - even I thought them strange!

Then the Cornishman, big and bear like, with a great black beard, who said he was a nationalist and knew about Caradoc's background, but refused to tell me any information other than Caradoc was a powerful warrior, and that a number of blood lines in Cornwall passed down the real history in the 'old' way, which I presumed meant by word of mouth - like the Bards!

So you see, with your story as well it has fired my resolve to find out more. I will be visiting the chapel very soon. My wife and I took a little scouting mission and found Ladye Park House. Lynn suggested being as we were there we might as well knock and introduce ourselves. Strangely, although there were several cars parked in the front of the house and a white dog watching us from the window, no one answered. After several attempts "at waking the dead" we thought it would be better to give them a ring. By the way, the atmosphere was totally still, and calm, warm and friendly. It felt very peaceful.

The official opening of the mural went very well; it was an enjoyable experience. By chance the mayor who did the honours was Jean Reece and her daughter and son in law used to be caretakers at Lady Park. Great coincidence. They left because of strange happenings. Do you know what sort of happenings have been going on there? No one has actually said what!

As I said on the telephone to you, my mural should not have been done really only events overtook what was planned. It's almost like a net of events has been cast and is definitely pulling me into the centre, actually I should not say I, more like us, **our** paths have joined and for a while we must walk together with the same aim.

Yours sincerely
David

Above: A pilgrimage banner which hangs in the
Church of Our Lady and St Neot, Liskeard

Below: Hands clasped in prayer at the Shrine

Chaptra Dewdhek

(Chapter Twelve)
Dehwelans dhe bark an Arloedhes
Return to Ladye Park

Just one month after the ESBVM pilgrimage to Ladye Park another was reported in the West Briton and other local newspapers.

Each year the Diocese of Arundel and Brighton organises an ecumenical walking pilgrimage to a place, a shrine or an area exploring a particular theme, angle or aspect of their faith and Christian heritage. They find, year after year, the amazing personal and community value of going on a pilgrimage as their medieval forebears did, where the journey, walking, laughing, sharing, praying, singing, etc. are as important as the arrival at the destination. Every day they worship together as a Christian Community, not only journeying together but also growing together. They stop to pray in churches they pass, experiencing the wealth of Christian tradition in the land, and for lunch they stop at an inn or pub. They sleep in church, school and community halls.

For 1998 they decided upon the Saint Michael's Mount Pilgrimage, walking for fifteen days from 15th August to 30th August from Plymouth to St Michael's Mount. Their stops included ancient standing stones, Holy Wells and churches of all denominations. On day two the eighty or so pilgrims walked from Launceston to Liskeard. Somehow information about the lost shrine had filtered through to them and, never being a group to pass by a place of religious significance, they decided to make the ancient shrine site their first "God stop" of Day 3 on their way to Fowey.

After a service at Liskeard's Catholic Church of Our Lady and St. Neot, the front markers made their way ahead along Old Road followed by the rest of the party to the top of the "Mass Path." It was no doubt the first time since the Reformation that such a large group of pilgrims had descended the rocky path - other pilgrimages had begun from the lane below to allow for the old and the infirm, but as a membership requirement for this pilgrimage was that all should be " over 15 years of age and fit enough to walk an average of 16 miles a day" this presented no problem. The day was hot and sunny and the trees and shrubs overhanging the path gave welcome shade. Eventually they emerged into the sunlight again at the former shrine to pray for Christian Unity and sing the special pilgrimage hymn.

Permission had been granted by the owners for everyone to gather on the lawn in front of the house and beside the Baptistery. Unlike pilgrims of old, these had to carry neither food nor drink with them as a "luggage and refreshment van" was organised to go ahead and meet them at every stop. After a short talk by one of the members on the history of the shrine, including the story of Kerrid and her link with Ker who is represented by a Bee, the van drew up. Someone had realised the suitability of having the nectar of the gods and poets at this historical spot and to the delight and surprise of everyone, the customary water was supplemented by bottles of mead, which they sipped as they wandered the hallowed grounds, all with their own individual thoughts. Some dwelt on the many pilgrims who had passed that way in the past, some enjoyed being part of continuous history, some secretly wondered whether healings still took place there as a result of prayer and others laughed and joked as they bathed their feet, blistered from two days of walking, in the cool water of the running stream, before everyone set off for the next destination refreshed in body and spirit.

To this walking group, the visit to Ladye Park was just one of many places of interest in their two week long journey, but in terms of the history of the shrine it was an important stepping stone on the way to the "Return", which Our Lady was alleged to have requested - it was the second organised pilgrimage in less than two months. Whether or not David Whittley, the mural painter and artist, was aware of this is unknown, but when he contacted Sister 13 to tell her the painting she had commissioned was completed, he told her he had named it "Return to Ladye Park". It was agreed she would travel down to collect it, which she did early in November.

She had given him a completely free rein as to the composition of the painting, only saying it should be based on his mural painting of Our Lady of the Park. She was not disappointed. The artist had attached his own interpretation to it:

RETURN TO LADYE PARK
The painting is a symbol of the resurrection of the chapel and the return of Our Lady to the Park.
INTERPRETATION
The border represents the Celtic origins of the shrine. The design itself is a symbol of life, with its complicated journey between earthly life and spirituality. This is also reflected by the colours, the green of earth and the gold of the spirit, which forms the path to the chapel.

Top centre are the three white roses, the Holy Trinity, flanked by the design of fish, the symbol of the spread of Christianity, moving outward to the meeting of the old religions and the new, which embrace and become one path leading to the entrance of the garden.

The spirit of Our Lady fills the garden and all that enter with love and light. The dove and white roses all bring peace. The tree is a symbol of the union of body and spirit, with the fruits of knowledge and the blossom of eternal life.

The lily and the bees are a reminder of "Kerrid" the old goddess of love and eternal youth to whom the shrine was originally dedicated.

David

Sister 13 remarked on the outstanding serenity of the figure of Our Lady. "I'm glad you mentioned that," said David. "Even my daughter who is my strongest critic and rarely likes anything I paint said the same thing, but it wasn't originally going to be like that."

And then he proceeded to tell an extraordinary story.

He was delighted to be given the commission. It was a subject he definitely wanted to paint. He knew his subject matter and yet something kept stopping him. The problems were minor and merely artistic ones, such as being unable to find the correct paint or the correct brushes and then the size was wrong, but eventually he had overcome the difficulties and he saw a whole day in front of him, when he would have the house to himself and he knew he could settle down to the painting. As an artist, he explained, he always has the picture of what he wants to paint in his mind's eye before beginning. This is not a vision, but he can see the complete picture with all its detail in front of him. It does not usually evolve as he goes along, although small details may change. On this particular occasion he could see Our Lady clearly. Then suddenly something happened, which in spite of his background of Marine Commandos and the Merchant Navy frightened him, as he had never been frightened before. The figure of Our Lady in his mind's eye began to change, first the face turned into a skull, then her garments began to change until the figure looked to him like a skeleton clothed in a wedding dress, complete with veil and tiara. He felt petrified. He did not know what to do, so he did something he had never done in his life. He did not regard himself as a Christian, but he began to say the Our Father. He did not know why, but he felt that somehow this could help him and then he saw the figure changing until it was Our Lady again, but this time much more serene and beautiful than in his original picture. This he knew was how he must paint her and that was the portrayal in "Return to Ladye Park". He himself became calm and peaceful once more and from then on, all went smoothly as he happily painted the rest of the picture.

It is interesting to note, at this point, that David Whittley had never seen Margaret Pollard's picture "La Vierge à la Porcelaine", but some time later when this story was being relayed to a Jewish gentleman, he remarked that in poor light, because Our Lady's face is white and her hair black in 'La Vierge', the face could almost be taken as a skull and her full flowing draperies, veil and tiara were slightly reminiscent of a wedding gown.

Before Sister 13 left, David said that there was one thing he would like her to do, if she could before returning home with the picture and that was to take it to Ladye Park, just for a visit. This seemed a very strange request, but she said that if that was what he wanted, she could do so the following morning before driving back to London.

The caretaker's number was in her diary, so she rang and rather embarrassed explained the situation. She said she would merely walk around the grounds with it and so hopefully not cause any disruption of their taking children to school, etc. Permission was willingly given so the next morning, she drove to Ladye Park. The weather was a typical, fine Cornish drizzle but David had assured her the day before, that this would not harm the painting. Feeling very awkward, she took the picture from the car and then wondered what to do with it. What did David mean by taking it there on a visit. Was standing on the bridge at the entrance to the garden sufficient? Perhaps she should take a photo of the painting at Ladye Park as a proof that she had been there with it. Yes! That would be a good idea so she propped the painting up and took out her brand new Olympus camera. She had only purchased it at the beginning of the week and had taken three photos on the first film without any problem. However, when she went to take a photo of the painting, she could not get the camera to work. At first she thought she must have left the shutter open and run down the battery. It was not that, so in the end she said to herself, "So much for modern cameras with all their gadgets, I'll return to my old faithful 'Point and snap'." She still had her original in the car complete with film, so went to fetch it. Unfortunately that too seemed to have a flat battery because nothing happened, when she tried with that camera so she gave up and very self- consciously walked around the grounds carrying the painting. She hoped against hope that no-one was looking out the window at her. They would think she was mad walking around in the rain carrying a painting. She stopped and held it over the stream, and suddenly it was as though she was seeing it for the first time, but it was also as though the water in the stream was flowing straight into the picture and then the stream was becoming the picture of Mary. As she looked again, she saw that in the painting Mary is rising from the water as a fountain. She is the fountain. Then Sister 13 noticed the beautiful rose in Mary's hands. She was holding it with such love and care, and into Sister's mind came the countless prayers said on rosaries and she knew that the rose Mary was holding was a symbol of each and every prayer that had been and would ever be said. It is lovingly received on behalf of her Son.

A little taken aback by the sudden clarity with which she had viewed the picture she decided that enough was enough. She had visited Ladye Park with the picture as requested and would now drive home with it.

On the way home she could not but ponder on her experience that morning. She had a feeling that something had happened but nothing had. Two cameras had failed to work but that was no doubt coincidence. She had had an 'insight' into the painting - but was that just because she had not studied it properly the day before? She just did not know.

Ynkleudhva Myghtern Arthur?
Burial Place of King Arthur?

When by September 1998, Sister 13 had had no luck in finding a purchaser for Ladye Park she contacted the owners and suggested they put it in the hands of an agent. The events over the last few months had anyway proved to her that Our Lady obviously did have things in hand, and so there was, as Kate had said there would be, no need for her to worry herself any more. Nevertheless several of those who had shown interest in the property continued to keep in contact with her via telephone, e-mail and letter, asking for details and sometimes making suggestions such as the possibility of it being purchased as a co-operative, so at the beginning of October it was decided to have a meeting of all those interested to perhaps come up with a way forward. The response to this was good and interested parties travelled from as far apart as Birmingham and Cornwall. One planned to fly in from Jersey, but this was cancelled at the last moment. The small party contained a good cross section of professionals as well as those who described themselves as lovers of Our Lady and the Holy Spirit. All were Christian.

After much discussion the general consensus was that the best way forward was for it to be purchased by some form of religious trust rather than by an individual owner, who would need to sell at some point There was much deliberation as to how this would be funded and bearing in mind Dr Pollard's National Trust connections, it was thought it could be run on the same lines. Donations would come from lovers of Our Lady and donors would become members of the trust. There was much banter as to a name for the trust. Suggestions ranged from "The Ecumenical Trust of Our Lady" to "The Christ through Mary Trust."

John, a down to earth accountant, reminded the assembled group that although gathering the funds for the purchase could be a problem, ongoing financing of the project would be even more difficult, so the next discussion was concerned with proposals for the use of the house and grounds once purchased by the trust.

National Trust properties are rented to people, who have connections with the property or who are in sympathy with the aims of the Trust. It was suggested that this would be the same for Ladye Park. It could be rented to a small religious or lay community - or even a Christian family. With further ideas gained from the National Trust a suggestion was made that the out-buildings could be converted into a religious book and art & craft centre. The books could be second hand as well as new and could cover all Christian subjects, including Celtic Christianity and early Cornish saints. The Cornish miracle plays were also mentioned. Cornwall is renowned for its arts and crafts, but those sold would only be articles with a Christian theme (e.g. paintings with Biblical texts attached, religious items in pottery, etc.) and all would be handmade. They could be sold either on a 10% commission basis, or a "stall" could be hired out, or just advertising space could be rented out with artists, showing one item with photographs of others which are available to order.

The ideas came thick and fast and included a small tea shop for thirsty pilgrims, who had left their car in Liskeard to travel on foot via the Mass Path. At times their enthusiasm and imaginations ran away with them, resulting in many impossible suggestions such as the trust purchasing Webbs Hotel, a wonderful Edwardian building in the centre of Liskeard, which had been empty for some time and had become a bit of an eyesore. They thought it could be made into a multi-faith spiritual centre or a pilgrim hostel.

Inevitably the discussion turned back to the purpose of any trust, which might be formed. It must surely have spiritual aims not material ones. The group were moving away from their whole reason for being there - to try and discover what Our Lady meant by the words "Take me back to Liskeard" and to fulfil her wish. Pictures of Fatima and Lourdes came to mind, but they all felt this shrine was not to be like them. Those who had attended the annual Catholic New Dawn Charismatic Conference or Spring Harvest wanted it to have that type of atmosphere. Some suggested an 'Alpha' (evangelisation) centre, but others wanted something much more contemplative, perhaps a religious art gallery, exhibiting paintings such as those of Elizabeth Wang, whose works represent aspects of truths, which have come to her in prayer. Then Keigwyn, who was one of the group members, asked the question "Who would the shrine be for? Catholics? Christians of all denominations? Members of other religions and none? Searchers? What would they expect to find there?"

The Catholics in the group said without a doubt they would want the Blessed Sacrament and the celebration of Mass. The others immediately said that this would of its very essence exclude them and the subject of respect and reverence came up. The Blessed Sacrament, which Catholics regard as Christ Himself, has a different significance for other Christians. They therefore decided that if Ladye Park were to become a centre for peace and unity, it must be non-denominational and yet everyone must feel they have a stake in it. Our Lady spreading her mantle of love and comfort must be the unifying factor. Those who visit must be those, who wish to know more about her, whatever their background. Being on the outskirts of Liskeard, rather than in the town they decided was ideal. Catholics could celebrate the Mass in their parish church either before or after any pilgrimage, but as an integral part of it. Protestants could begin with services in their own churches if they so desired. Other religions or organisations could do the same if they wished, but all would meet at Ladye Park to honour Mary, the most perfect woman who ever lived, now reigning as Queen of Heaven.

The meeting had begun at 10.30am on a Saturday. Some five hours later (interspersed with cups of coffee and other refreshments) the group reluctantly admitted that they were no further forward than they had been at the beginning. It had been a fascinating day, meeting each other, airing their views, making suggestions, but no firm decisions had been made which would further Our Lady's cause. It looked as though they must just wait patiently to see what she had in store.

They did not have long to wait and Our Lady certainly seemed to be backing the idea that she wanted to be part of everyone's lives - not just those of Christians.

In January 1999, Ladye Park was sold. The new owner Gwyneth did not regard herself as a Christian. She said that the nearest name to her beliefs was New Age. To many Christians this was at first a great disappointment. They could not understand that in spite of all their prayers, Our Lady seemed to have missed out once more. In fact, it was thought that the situation was preferable before the house was sold, because at least pilgrimages had been permitted then, but they need not have worried. From the moment Gwyneth and Anna, with whom she originally shared the house, moved in they could not have been more welcoming to lovers of Our Lady. They immediately agreed to the ESBVM pilgrimage going ahead in the Summer and accepted Mike Jennings, the ESBVM secretary, Sister 13 and Pegasus as friends at liberty to visit or phone at any time. Sister 13 was in Cornwall not long after they moved in and called on them. They had an incredible story to tell.

Gwyneth had been looking for a place in Cornwall and soon after receiving details from the agent, she asked her friend Anna to call. Neither of them knew anything about the history of the site, but as soon as Anna walked towards the house she said she became aware of it being surrounded by monks walking in and out of the bush at the left hand side of the house. It was only later that she was told of the blocked up chapel door and that monks had once lived there. Sister 13 did not know what to make of this revelation. Half of her did not wish to believe it. She felt for some reason she should not, but she remembered the monk she had seen in Sheila Richards' photo, so she decided to keep an open mind. Far from the idea of sharing the house with monks, who were not really there, putting her off, as it might some people; for Gwyneth, this idea together with Kerrid's well of eternal youth being situated in the grounds was the reason she decided to purchase. Her intention was to open it up as a place of healing via aromatherapy, herbs, kinaesiology and other complimentary medicines. Like Sheila Richards, Anna and Gwyneth did not regard these apparitions as ghosts. When questioned more closely they explained that they "resonated on their same wavelengths". They also, like Sheila, admitted that they could become aware of other beings almost anywhere, but they found it particularly easy to tune in at Ladye Park. There was nevertheless a difference between Sheila Richards' Christian beliefs and attitude and their New Age beliefs.

On future visits Sister 13 heard other stories about the monks, how they had had conversations with them, how they even answered questions. They seemingly told that they had not lived at Ladye Park but in a monastery over the hill, that there had been between ten and twelve of them and they had been there in the 11th century. They had names. One of them was named Brother Juniper, whom they said was delightful, of aristocratic background and loved herbs! Sister 13 took all this with a pinch of salt. She could not but recall her childhood catechism classes concerning divination and magic, but there were no attempts to 'unveil' the future or conjure these beings up. It sounded as though, in their minds, they were present and real so she left it at that.

Then on one occasion a few months later, when Sister 13 was visiting, Anna told her that one of the monks that morning had given her a message which she did not understand. It was "Benedict means Blessings."

Sister 13 said nothing. Inwardly, however, she could not but wonder whether it was connected to a Sierra Leonian law student, Benedict, whom she had been sponsoring for the last few months. She had met him quite by accident the previous September, but she had grown so close to him he had become like the son she had never had. She did consider meeting him had been a blessing. Curious - but she still said nothing.

Although these strange stories of monks continued, both Gwyneth and Anna were very conscious of Our Lady's presence - not they said in the same way as the monks. They did not see her, but Anna in particular spoke of feeling Our Lady's cloak around her, protecting her. Later, after she had left Ladye Park, which she did before Gwyneth, Anna spoke of it as a time she would not have missed for anything, when she had felt privileged to have Our Lady's protection. She also admitted some of the monks were not good. Some were in fact evil, although not all. She said she was grateful for Our Lady's protection from the evil ones. Some like Brother Juniper, whom she had already mentioned were, charming. This set Sister 13 thinking of conversations she had had in the past with Dr Pollard of the presence of evil amongst good and the need to be able to discern the difference between God's civil service and Satan's. One of Kate's sayings had been "Leave God alone and Satan will leave you alone". Sister 13 found a verse from the Ladye Park pilgrimage hymn coming into her head.

"Set your foot upon the serpent,
Sinless Virgin, intercessor.
Wrap your veil about the lonely,
Clasp the sinner to your bosom:
Tell your Son the wine is failing,
Tell us how to do his bidding,
Queen of Martyrs! Tower of David!
Hear your children's song of praise.
Hayl Maria
Hayl Maria
Col orthyn warnas ow crya
Agan lelder owth-affya,
Hayl Marya lun a ras!

Why, she wondered should this come to mind? Then she realised it was because of the first line.

While living there, Gwyneth did many things for Our Lady. She planted Madonna lilies, she renovated the well and she cleared the old chapel area, often placing flowers in the niche in the old chapel wall. She tirelessly welcomed lovers of Our Lady, who made arrangements to call.

On one particular Saturday, Sister 13 and Pegasus had visited with a couple of pilgrims. Gwyneth invited them back in the evening for a glass of wine and a leisurely stroll around
    the grounds on what turned out to be a beautiful Summer's evening. They climbed up through the woods at the back, which Pegasus suggested would make a wonderful rosary way or calvary with stations of the cross which could be attached to trees along the path. Anna was there too, and among other things she spoke of a monk, who she said often stood by the fireplace in the house. She had it seems asked him his name and he had replied "Bedivere". For some reason she said she had felt she should ask Sister 13 whether she knew who that could be. Did she know of anyone of that name who had ever lived at Ladye Park? Did she know of any saint or monk of that name?" Sister 13 said she did not and the conversation continued no further.

That night however, Sister 13 could not resist looking up in Butler's lives of the saints and a few other places the name "Bedivere." She found nothing, so forgot the conversation until two year's later, when in the Cornish library at Redruth she was reading an old copy of Malory's "Morte d'Arthur". Although many people have a fascination with the story of King Arthur, Sister 13 had never thought very much about it, but as she read this legend in verse, she began to get shivers down her spine. She read how the mortally injured Arthur asked to be taken in a boat by the three queens to Avalon. She read of how the dying King did not want his loyal knight, Sir Bedivere to travel further with him. She read of how upset the knight had been and eventually rode through the night to the "Hermitage", where he saw "a hermit" kneeling in prayer over a newly dug grave. On asking the monk whom he had buried there, the hermit replied that he did not know. He reported how at midnight three ladies dressed in black had brought a corpse. They had given a large donation and asked him to bury the body. Sir Bedivere told the hermit that he was convinced this was his Lord and Master, King Arthur, whom he had vowed to serve all his life and now he would continue to serve him and remain at the hermitage where his king lay for the rest of his days.

The poem did not say that the hermitage was at Avalon, only that King Arthur had sailed for Avalon, but as Sister 13 connected in her mind the name "Bedivere' with the monk whom Anna had mentioned and the 'Sir Bedivere' in the legend, she remembered that the Cornish word for 'apple' was 'aval'. Could Avalon mean 'orchard'? If so, could it refer to the orchard at Ladye Park mentioned so often in old records? In which case, what could be more plausible than for the dying Christian King Arthur to ask to float down to Avalon, the orchard at the Shrine of Our Lady of the Park, where a priest (the hermit) would be ready to give him the Last Rites, to bury him, and pray for his soul? The river would doubtless have been wider at the time.

As thoughts came nineteen to the dozen into Sister 13's mind, she recalled a conviction David Whittley had mentioned as having whilst painting "Return to Ladye Park." He had told her that a strong feeling had come over him that something was buried at Ladye Park under a reddish slab, which he thought might be slate. He had explained that he had had an intuition, that the discovery of whatever was buried there would bring publicity to the shrine, which in turn would mark a return to the days when Liskeard would once more be a place of pilgrimage. At the time Sister 13 had taken little notice of this 'prophecy.' She knew there was a legend that when the King's men had been sent to plunder the churches at the Dissolution, they stopped with their horses for a drink at an inn in central Liskeard. The story went on to tell that, by the time they arrived at the shrine of Our Lady of the Park two hours later, the church silver had all disappeared and has never been found to this day. Sister 13 had thought that perhaps, if anything, there might be buried treasure there, but she had soon forgotten this idea. Now however she began to think back to David's words. Could the something buried be 'someone' and could it be King Arthur? The idea was almost too mind- blowing to contemplate, but she also remembered reading in another book, she could not place which one, that the dying King Arthur was supposed to have started his final journey to Avalon from Dozmary Pool. This is a mile-long sheet of water high on Bodmin Moor. Not only was that close enough to Ladye Park for one to easily imagine there had once been a connecting stream, but Margaret Pollard had often mentioned the lake with its mysterious atmosphere, saying she was convinced that the name meant 'Dowry of Mary Pool' and being so near to Our Lady's shrine there must be a connection.

These thoughts almost became too much for sister 13, for she knew that if Ladye Park turned out to be the burial place of King Arthur there was no knowing what the future could bring. However, she decided not to continue with this line of thinking, mindful of how Satan's civil service is very capable of laying false trails.

Above: Detail of teenager in David Whittley's mural,
wearing a sweatshirt imprinted with 'HOPE 2000'

Below: Interior of the Church of Our Lady and St Neot, Liskeard

Chaptra Trydhek

(Chapter Thirteen)
Profyans a lymnans-fos
Mural Proposal

As time went by, members of the original OLDG (Our Lady's Discussion Group) were intrigued to see how often the Blessed Virgin seemed to put a seal of approval on ideas they had discussed. Gwyneth's purchasing Ladye Park certainly seemed to be part of a larger plan and for the Catholics at least, the idea of them centring their devotion around the Mass in the parish church, was given a tremendous thumbs up by another "curious happening."

In May 1999 David Whittley was painting a mural at the Seaton Nature Reserve. As happened when he was painting the Liskeard mural he was often approached by passers-by asking him about his painting. On one such occasion a lady stood for a little while admiring his artistry and asking what other work he did. He told her and she then offered that she was on the committee of her local church, which was going through a complete refurbishment and they might be interested in some kind of mural to surround the crucifix on the rear wall of the chancel. He gave her his card and thought no more about it. The number of cards distributed compared to the number of commissions received is very small.

The following September David received a phone call from an Edmund Wilson, inviting him to come to the church, mainly to recommend a new colour scheme, with a mind to looking at the possibility of a mural.

David was very surprised to discover that the church concerned was none other than Liskeard Catholic Church, situated almost directly behind the Pig Meadow Lane Mural.

An appointment was made for late September and Edmund and David met as arranged in the car park, situated beside the church at seven in the evening. Edmund led the artist around to the side entrance and began to unlock the doors for him. David was not a churchgoer, but still had the idea in his mind that churches were havens open to all. He was saddened by the almost prison-like security which surrounded the church and felt what a poor reflection it was on the society of which he was part, that even churches now have to be bolted and barred.

As however they entered the aisle he said afterwards, "It gave me a lovely feeling of warmth and peace"

He saw a pleasant, clean-lined building, typical of late eighteenth century architecture. They both stood in front of the altar and Edmund showed him the wall at the rear of the chancel and the beautiful carving of Jesus on the crucifix, which would be surrounded by the mural.

Edmund had genuflected (the gesture of going down on one knee before the Blessed Sacrament) on entering, but David was unaware of the meaning of this custom or that the tabernacle is the most important item in a Catholic church, so merely observed and looked around, but despite his lack of knowledge he found his eyes being drawn towards the tabernacle. He describes what happened next in his own words.

"What attracted me was a kind of white light, actually within the wall is the best way I can explain it. The light took on the shape of an old man, dressed in robes of some sort. The entire figure was in a soft, white light. Not floating like a ghost but still within the wall, almost as if being projected on to it like a film screen. I was surprised and asked Edmund if he could see what I could see. "What can you see?" he asked, as he couldn't see anything. So I narrated to him what I was actually experiencing. The figure was fairly bent over the tabernacle. He turned and looked straight at me and seemed to be offering what I thought was the wall to me. At this I felt a huge amount of energy pouring into me which made the hairs stand up on the back of my head as if I was being gently electrocuted. Edmund still could not see the figure, but he certainly felt the electric atmosphere. As I watched this figure it gently faded out but I was telling Edmund everything I was experiencing at the time, so I do have a witness even though he did not see what I did. The rest of that evening I was greatly agitated with so much energy and

excitement."

On 7th October the church committee met with the artist and agreed that he should go ahead to design a mural for a fee and recommend a colour scheme for the church.

David was delighted with this commission, but the design proved a problem to him. He had not been able to forget the figure he had seen in the church the night of his visit. He did not know who it was, but imagined that as the church was called "Our Lady & St Neot's", it could have been St Neot. If this were the case, he felt he should include him as an integral part of the mural. He had a concept of what he wanted, but try as he might to include him in all kinds of ways, nothing would work. It was rare that his happened to him, but as he said himself, "I was in real trouble with this design"

In the end he decided he must take another trip to Liskeard on the pretext of taking measurements for the mural, but secretly hoping he would gain much needed inspiration and even catch another glimpse of "St. Neot".

Tuesday, 9th November 1999 was dark and rainy as he drove from Saltash to Liskeard. The headlights of the oncoming traffic were dazzling and at some stages blinding. Then, "Click!" It was as though something happened in his mind. He thought of Saint Paul, who was blinded by the light of God and then had a new understanding and changed his priorities completely. David had suddenly a new understanding and was starting to see a much fuller picture too. He knew without a doubt that the mural had to show in some way the transition that man's spirit must make from an earthly perspective to the full attainment of God's domain. Not having much of a Christian grounding or knowledge of the Bible, he checked with Edmund that he had remembered the story of St. Paul correctly and was on the right track.

Having returned home he immediately started designing. He had no problems with the design now. From the beginning he had wanted to incorporate the history of the church, which was built by the miners and was one of the first to be built once the restrictions on building Catholic churches were lifted.

From the Reformation onwards, it had been very difficult for the Cornish to accept the Church of England. Its insistence on the Book of Common Prayer being in English instead of Cornish all but destroyed their beloved Cornish language and with Catholicism forbidden, a Christian vacuum was formed making it an ideal conversion ground for Methodism in the mid 18th century. Amongst the miners however the Catholic religion during the times of Catholic persecution remained alive much longer, for they found that they could create chapels in the mines, hidden from view and thus undisturbed by the looters and desecrators. Here they could continue hearing Mass and receiving the Sacraments with the priest disguised as an ordinary miner. At first these chapels were no doubt adorned with statues and artefacts they had managed to rescue from the churches before the King's men arrived to confiscate them, but as time went by crucifixes and figures of saints would have no doubt been carved into the wooden pit props or hewn from stone.

An unexpected throwback to these times was reported in the "West Briton" - a Cornish newspaper - roundabout the same time as David Whittley was designing his mural. It reported that a mysterious carving of a Madonna and Child had been found near Trevaunance Cove in the village of St. Agnes. Inscribed next to the figures the word 'gaudete' meaning 'rejoice' could clearly be seen. The account suggested that it could have been washed from an underground altar in a mine shaft and went on to explain to its readers, how Cornwall had been a staunchly Catholic county and people held their Mass in secret and miners formed secret societies and built small altars in the mines. The finder a Mr Johnson believed it was a strange coincidence that he found it on the feast day of St Agnes, 21st January 1999. Catholics believed there was significance in the fact their parish church situated in Trevaunance Road, built in 1958 is named "Our Lady Star of the Sea." Mr Johnson said he was led to the spot where he found it, because he was attracted by a piece of driftwood standing upright in the sand. There was something strange about it. It looked like a finger pointing to something. He walked aimlessly forward and noticed it seemed to be pointing to another piece of wood. It was a 4ft piece of

English elm carved with the Madonna and Child. The article quoted the finder as saying,

"In the reign of Elizabeth I, the celebrating of the Roman Catholic Mass was outlawed and punishable by fines and imprisonment." He then went on to say that he thought the recent severe flooding and rainfall could have washed it from some underground altar, where she had been left, forgotten for the past 400 years.

David Whittley had not seen this report, but had been researching the history of Christianity in Cornwall.

The Catholic church in Liskeard, he discovered was built in 1863 by miners from the surrounding moorland. They had been worshipping in a little school-chapel since the ending of Catholic persecution, but there was an ever increasing congregation so a larger building was imperative. It was with all this background information that he made his preliminary drawing.

The design for the mural almost gives a stained- glass window effect from altar height to ceiling. The surround is two granite pillars painted in a *trompe l'oeil* style (meaning deceive the eye). The mural is divided into three horizontal sections with a middle column throughout. At the top of the column is a circle of light symbolising God Eternal. The light is directed down through the three levels and the overall impression is one of light and warmth radiating from heaven above down to earth. Central to the whole mural is the existing crucifix which is in the column of light at the middle level.

Beginning with the base level, at altar height we see on the right side the miners leaving the mines with their families, moving towards the light and away from darkness. Instead of pickaxes they carry crosses, symbols of their faith and that of their forefathers, who kept it alive in times of difficulty. The crosses are also a reminder of the Stations of the Cross, depicting how greatly Christ suffered on his way to crucifixion. The candles on the miners' helmets convey the light of hope which burns brightly even in the darkest places.

On the left side at this level can be seen rocks and stones strewn, some of which are dressed ready to be used for the church building. The miners and their families are the church as a people. It is at this earthly level that we come to understand that we are the church as a people. It is also at this earthly level that we come to understand that we are body, mind and spirit and that human life is a gradual learning process. It is a place where we grow to understand our unique position of being touched by the light of God and formed in his image. We experience from a human perspective attributes of God like Love, Mercy, Compassion, Peace, Truth, Glory, Grace and Forgiveness but this is nothing to how we will encounter them once the trappings of this earthly level are left behind. We need however to overcome human obstacles like fear and selfishness and to work together for the good of all humanity to reach the light.

The middle level is divided by the column of light radiating to earth. This is the light of God and it flows down through Christ on the cross, who is the link between heaven and earth. The light of God flows not only down but back up through Christ to the Father and Holy Spirit. Each side of the crucifix shows the transition between this world and the next. The confines of earthly bodies are left behind. In a symbolic way it shows the human spirit or soul gradually becoming aware of God. This is depicted by the different states of the figures that are in a kind of **flux**. Some are almost fully formed, others not. For some this is a Purgatory or purifying state for those who have not been drawn straight up by the light but here there are also God's spirits, the angels of the Lord, particularly near the column of light and the crucifix.

The top level, when examined is subdivided. The centre is God and this is the light eternal shining his love down. All around there are figures of almost pure light. They are complete. They have attained everlasting joy, having risen to the light and are at one with God. The circle of love is complete.

Very happy with this design David Whittley completed his commission by submitting it together with a plan for the redecoration of the church. It was well received and the decoration of the church went ahead according to his suggestion. However, it was decided by the church maintenance committee that any decision to go ahead with the mural would have to be postponed. The parish was only a very small one and their limited funds had other priorities. The external fabric of the building needed a great deal of repair and it was also discovered that the chancel wall, where the mural would have been painted had developed some serious cracks.

David Whittley accepted this and realised there had never been a promise that the mural would be commissioned. What baffled him however was why such a small parish should have even considered something as ambitious as a mural. He also could not wipe from his mind the experience he had had on his first visit to the church. Who or what was the figure and if it was some supernatural intervention why had he indicated the wall to him - as if to say, "Here it is"?

He pondered on this for some time and came to the conclusion that he was meant to paint this mural. He realised that the question of finance would always be a difficulty for such a small parish, so wondered how he could help solve the problem.

As an artist he had always relied on what he called "gut feelings" or an "inner knowledge." At this time he had a very strong feeling that the mural would be painted. It would not just be a pretty picture for the church parishioners, but it would become what he called a "teaching tool" He felt that the future would see the church, not locked and bolted as he had seen it but open wide to a much larger public. He saw it first as a jumping off point for a revival of spiritual fervour in Liskeard, spreading to the whole of Cornwall and even further afield. America came very much into his mind and he wondered whether there was any way that expatriate Cornishmen could be asked to contribute to a fund. He had had no connection with the OLDG but he had heard of the pilgrimages, which had been held to Ladye Park and how they had attracted members of all Christian denominations and none and he felt that the Church of Our Lady and St Neot, being next to a car park would make an ideal start or end point. Meditation on the mural at these times could be an integral part.

With all these thoughts churning around in his mind he decided that there would be a good case for applying for funding from South West Arts, the agent for the Arts Council and Lottery funding for the South West.

Realising that he should at least notify the church that he was applying for any available funds, he made a quick phone call which he thought would be a courtesy call. To his disappointment the response he received was such that he felt it had been decided that whatever the circumstances the mural would not go ahead.

That night, he and his wife, discussed the situation with a Catholic friend. She was not from Liskeard parish and had not seen the design plans, although she had been privy to the alleged sighting of 'St Neot.' She tried to put herself into the position of a member of a parish council considering a mural for a Catholic church. She was worried that it might distract from the most fundamental doctrine of the Catholic Church, that of the Real Presence. She reminded David of how he had said he had seen Edmund on his first visit "bobbing down." She explained that this was a mark of respect, similar to a bow before royalty, made by Catholics when the Blessed Sacrament was present. " I" she said, "would be worried in case the mural became the focus of attention instead of the tabernacle. The one thing people are always accusing Catholics of is worshipping pictures and statues instead of God. We don't adore anyone except God. Every picture or statue in a Catholic church is there for one purpose and that is to help visitors raise their heart and mind to God present there in an extra special way. If therefore there was going to be mural behind the altar I would want to make absolutely sure that its subject matter would lead people to focus on the Blessed Sacrament and not some distraction."

David was silent for a moment and then he put his hand to his head and said,

"What a fool I've been. What an ignoramus. I see it so clearly now! I thought that figure in the church was pointing to the wall. Of course he wasn't! He was pointing to the tabernacle which is on the wall! He was trying to warn me that no matter what I did it must enhance and not detract from it, but now I know there will be no problem. The design was never written in stone and always open to change. What I will do now is just make a few changes at the earth level. Obviously the miners who were Catholic would know the importance of the tabernacle for what it contains. They would be genuflecting to the Real Presence too. I will put one of the miners on one knee before the light which is streaming from Heaven and perhaps have a symbolic tabernacle in it for of course the Blessed Sacrament is obviously part of the light and part of God."

David knew after this conversation that he must contact the Liskeard church again to explain his enlightenment and that with slight changes he truly believed it would reach out "to open doors" for people who might not usually visit a Catholic church, but once there, they would experience the same warmth and peace that he had on his first visit and become aware of God, some for the first time.

In January 2001 he received a letter saying that the parish had made a final decision against the mural for three reasons:

1. Many members of the parish preferred the plain white wall as it helped them to focus on other religious items.

2. There were even more cracks in the wall where the mural was to be painted.

3. The parish did not have the wherewithal to finance the project.

The artist was disappointed that no mention had been made of his thoughts of how it could reach out to those who do not usually go into a church or his applying for funding, but he understood that it was their church and not his and decisions had to be made in the light of what was thought best for the parish at that time. He was grateful to have been given the opportunity of such a wonderful inspiration and would keep the plans for - who knew what in the future?

Fenten nowydh a omdhiskwa
A new spring Appears

The 1999 ESBVM pilgrimage to Ladye Park was again held on 11th July. The weather could not have been more in contrast to the previous year. The pilgrims gathered on a blistering hot summer day. The flavour of this year's event was decidedly Cornish which was very appropriate as it coincided with a five day march from Bodmin to Exeter of Cornish folk remembering the Cornish Prayer Book Rebellion of 1549. A banner displaying the Kernewek (Cornish) words "Hayl Maria Leun a Ras" (Hail Mary Full of Grace) was added to the original collection held aloft as the pilgrims made their way once more along the leafy lane to the entrance of Ladye Park, saying the rosary and singing hymns. Whereas the previous year the laurel and other bushes meeting to form an arch in the area of the old altar gave shelter from the torrential rain, this year they gave protection from the burning sun. Cornish Bard Philip Knight said the Hayl Maria in Cornish and the short service ended with a beautiful rendering of his Cornish song "Maria Wynn A Gernow" (Our Lady of Cornwall)

The owner, Gwyneth welcomed the group unreservedly. She spoke glowingly of the incredible peace she found living in the valley and then announced the most wonderful surprise. Two weeks earlier, she had been walking in the garden and noticed a new spring had appeared in the grounds. She had had the water analysed and it was the purest of Cornish spring water. To many this was reminiscent of the springs at shrines such as Lourdes and Fatima and a stamp of approval as it were from Our Lady. As the pilgrims wandered the lawns they drank from the spring, so welcome on this hot day, and prayed that it was a sign of hope for the future.

Two weeks later, the aspirations of some were dashed. The water from the spring became contaminated. It was not known whence the pollution stemmed. Many ideas were put forward but a comment was made that it seemed a coincidence that the spring, which had appeared somewhat miraculously at Truro during the building of the church, had also become polluted. Some wondered in these days of pure water becoming a commodity and sold, whether Our Lady had forestalled any such idea by ensuring that there would be no market for it. Others fancifully suggested that the spring had arisen purely for the ESBVM pilgrimage, officially affirming Our Lady's pleasure that pilgrimages had recommenced, but that the time had not yet come for the full restoration of the shrine. When that happened the spring it was thought would become pure and clean once more. The true reason is, of course, unknown, a great deal of work had been carried out in the grounds in order to lay a new cess pit, so no doubt this had caused water pathways to become redirected and perhaps a contaminated underground stream crossed the path of the source as it rose through the ground. Whatever the reason the spring remains and is a reminder of the 1999 ESBVM pilgrimage.

Gwyneth, the then owner of Ladye Park, had purchased the property with the express intention of opening it up as some form of alternative health centre, but unfortunately for her, the business did not get off the ground. She had had a great deal of expense in renovating the property, but when she found that the expected income was not materialising, she decided to cut her losses and put it back on the market. This she did at Easter in the year 2000.

Although lovers of Our Lady had been dubious, when Gwyneth had first purchased the property for fear of her refusing entry to pilgrimages, they were now very disconcerted that she was moving on, since she had been such a welcoming owner. To their amazement and delight she made it known that she was so convinced that eventually Ladye Park would return to being a permanent shrine to Our Lady that she intended asking her solicitor to include a new covenant permitting at least one pilgrimage to the ancient shrine site to take place every year between the months of May and October. In actual fact when it came to it, her solicitor explained this would not be possible, but there is no doubt that she would have built this into any contract had she possibly been able to do so. Our Lady had indeed touched her during her time at Ladye Park.

When Ladye Park had been put on the market in 1999 devotees of the shrine felt that they must do all in their power to find a suitable purchaser, on this occasion there was a strange calm amongst them. It was generally believed that Our Lady had proved that she had the matter in hand, so it was just a case of waiting. There was however one more meeting of the OLDG, which was held on 6th August 2000. There was no agenda and it was more a meeting of old and new friends. The members had changed slightly with a couple having moved abroad and one or two new members having joined.

Sister 13 had recently attended the New Dawn Conference for Charismatic Catholics at Walsingham. Whilst there, Fr Gwinnell announced that on the 8th October 2000 the Pope would be consecrating the world and the third millennium to Our Blessed Lady. He said that Our Lady's statue from Fatima would be in Rome for three days and that the Pope had asked that there should be "echo" prayers all around the world in as many Marian shrines as possible. Fr Gwinnell then went on to exhort the delegates at the conference to think of any shrine that might be near their home and not to wait for someone else to arrange something, but to organise an event themselves. Ladye Park had obviously come into Sister 13's mind and now she mentioned it to the gathered group. It was agreed unanimously that it would be wonderful, if somehow the echo of prayers said at the Shrine of Our Lady of the Park in the past could be transferred in to the "echo prayers" the Pope was requesting in the year 2000, but it was realised that with the uncertainty of who would be owning the property on that day, it was regrettably not feasible to plan anything. They still felt that even if they could not assemble physically they should as a group try to do something to mark the occasion. After much discussion it was agreed that there was only one thing which could be done - to pray and to ask others to pray " that our Lady will make known her will as regards the re-establishment of a permanent shrine at Liskeard and that if it be her will that a celebration might take place there on October 8th 2000." The name Liskeard was purposely used instead of Ladye Park as it was remembered Our Lady was alleged to have said "Take me back to Liskeard" It was also decided at this time that the group would re-name themselves "Prayer Friends of the Lost Shrine."

Little did that small group realise at the time how fast the "Prayer Friends" would grow - that within weeks there would be members all over the world or how positively their prayers would be answered.

In order to save on stationery and postage, it had been agreed that all communications between "Prayer Friends" should be by e-mail. Anyone not on the internet was asked to find someone who was, whose e-mail address they could give for occasional communication. It was thought that in this day and age there would be very few people with no access to a computer. It was also decided that anyone who prayed should be given feed back after 8th October, even if it was only to say. "Thanks for praying - Our Lady must have diverted all the prayers to Rome!" However, that was not the message, which was sent!

Claire, a member of the original group, had recently acquired a computer with access to the internet and had also attended a beginners course on the subject at the local community college. Anxious to put her new found skills into practice she set up an e-mail account for the Lost Friends with the address "Lostshrine@hotmail.com" and at the same time logged onto "Indcatholicnews." Seeing a request for articles, news of general interest, or details of organisations, she sent off an e-mail asking, if publicity could be given to "Prayer Friends of the Lost Shrine." Josephine Siedlecka, the editor replied immediately, most interested in the shrine and saying she would write an item. This she did and it appeared on the Indcatholic news web site on 11th August 2000. As a result of that article another was written in "The Tablet", and from then on e-mail requests for more information arrived thick and fast from all over the world. Several requests came from religious and missionaries, pleased to be able to join an e-mail organisation. Many, although not all, who replied, had connections with Cornwall or were Marian enthusiasts. All were asked to pray until 8th October. No set prayers were suggested or frequency. They were informed that they would receive an e-mail after that date informing them of the future for the "Prayer Friends."

Until Sister 13 had attended the New Dawn Conference, the proposed consecration of the new millennium to the Blessed Virgin seemed to be a well-kept secret in that she had heard nothing about it, but during the month of September publicity for the event seemed to gain momentum. She heard that the Pope had called for a novena (nine days of prayer) leading up to the Feast of Our Lady of the Rosary and the entrustment of the third millennium to Mary. She did not bother to mention this to any of the "Prayer friends of the Lost Shrine" as she assumed any who would pray would already be doing so. She had heard no more about the Ladye Park sale or non-sale as the case might be.

Then on the 21st September, she received a phone call from Gwyneth informing her that Ladye Park had been sold, that the new owners had told her they were Christians and they would be moving in on 29th September. Sister 13 could hardly believe her ears. Anyone who announces he is Christian is usually a practising one and it seemed they were moving in on the very day that Catholics all over the world were beginning their novena. She was desperate to find out more but had no idea how she could. She did not have long to wait. The next morning a surprise telephone call came from Michael Jennings, the secretary of the Cornish ESBVM. He too had heard the news and had not only made contact with the new owners but had been invited by them to tea in the home they would be leaving! They were indeed very strong Christians who believed that they were being "called" by God to move to Ladye Park. They knew nothing about its Marian history and were not at first particularly interested. Coming from an Anglican tradition in which Mary had played little part, they said that if they were given a rosary they would not know what to do with it. Nevertheless, they were certainly very great devotees of her Son and the Holy Spirit and had been running Alpha groups (evangelisation groups run by some Christian denominations) for some years. They were completely committed to spreading the name of Jesus throughout Cornwall. Michael explained, he had told them he and other Catholics did not adore or worship Mary, they just loved her and handed their prayers over to her for her Son. He felt they understood, but what thrilled him most was that they said they were very happy for the ESBVM Ladye Park pilgrimage already arranged for June 2001 to go ahead. He was positive that these two new owners were specially chosen by Jesus and his Mother to be custodians of the shrine and the future would unfurl the full plan.

There seemed to be one other startling proof from "Our Lady of Lovely Surprises" that the purchase was part of her plan. On the first Sunday of October, traditionally known as "Rosary Sunday", the new owners held a prayer and praise service for more than 30 people in their new home, Ladye Park to dedicate it and their lives there to spreading the Word of God. This day was chosen purely because it was two days after they moved in, certainly not because they were aware of the significance of the day and it is quite likely that if they had known, they might have had second thoughts about it, being involved in a totally 'Jesus' based group at the time. It had originally been planned that an Anglican minister should take the service, but being Harvest Festival Day he was needed at his local church. A retired Methodist minister was delighted when at the last minute he was invited to step into the breach, particularly as only the day before he had prepared a homily on Mary in preparation for a talk at Christmas, which had been promptly cancelled! He was in possession of notes he thought he would be unlikely to use, so hearing of the history of his old friends' new home he introduced the assembled group to Mary, to many for the first time.

Wherever Mary is, there the Holy Spirit is too and there was no doubt that He was present at Ladye Park that afternoon and as the words of the hymn "Spirit of the Living God, Fall afresh on us" rang out, a surge of emotion could be felt. David Whittley's mural portraying a teenager wearing a sweatshirt bearing the emblem of a dove, which is the symbol of the Holy Spirit, surrounded by H.O.P.E. 2000, came to mind for at least one of the group who prayed that this would be the beginning of a Spiritual revival in Cornwall.

The Prayer Friends of the Lost Shrine could not have been more thrilled with the result of their prayers An announcement was made in the Catholic Southwest newspaper and on Indcatholicnews web site to this effect and all members were e-mailed with the wonderful news and with a further request to pray

"that the new owners of Ladye Park be blessed and guided in all they try to do for the Lord and that all Christians in Liskeard can unite as friends in Christ so that their town, with the help of Mary, can once more become a beacon for Christianity throughout Cornwall and eventually the whole country."

Taklow kothhes yw nowydhys
Things grown old are made new

Satisfied that the ball was now definitely in Our Lady's court, Sister 13 made no further contact with the new owners over the next few months. At Christmas she heard the sad news that Mike Jennings, who had been so instrumental in reviving regular pilgrimages to Ladye Park was suffering from terminal cancer. His faith was strong. He knew that this meant the time was coming for him to move on to pastures new and felt that soon his beloved Mary would be introducing him to her son in person, something his spirit had longed for much of his life. Nevertheless the human side of him wanted to remain on this earth as long as possible, especially as he would be leaving behind his much loved wife, Marion and teenage daughters. He availed himself of all treatment possible and continued to plan for the future, including making arrangements for the Ladye Park pilgrimage in June, but his Lord obviously had other plans and within three months he was called to his heavenly reward.

Early one morning a couple of weeks before he died, Mike rang Sister 13 and was obviously feeling very emotional but also excited. His voice was barely audible. However, he had something he was desperate to tell her. That morning, whilst praying he had been given what he described as "a picture in prayer" He saw himself sitting in a vehicle drawn by three horses. Sitting up high with him, at the front of the cab, were Sister 13 and Cornish-speaking Bard Philip Knight. Each of them held the reins of one of the horses. On the front he could clearly see the word TROIKA and the horses were hurtling at break-neck speed towards Ladye Park.

This 'picture' meant a great deal to Mike. He felt that as a *Troika* is a Russian three-horse cart there must be a link with the alleged words, "You have been a good cab-horse bringing others to me", spoken in Russian by Our Lady to Dr Margaret Pollard in 1955. He presumably took this to be an acknowledgement that he was continuing Margaret Pollard's work of spreading knowledge of Ladye Park. He could not stay on the phone long as he became very breathless, but he was obviously full of joy.

Sister 13 found it hard to know what to make of this revelation. The experience had brought pleasure to Mike, so she was pleased, but she could not feel that it had any significance for her, so put the conversation to the back of her mind and only retrieved it on hearing the news of Mike's promotion to glory.

Whilst speaking to Philip Knight soon after the news of the death was announced, he remarked that Mike had mentioned there was something he had wanted to tell him, but he never had. Sister 13 recounted the story of the *TROIKA* emphasising how much it had meant to Mike and suggesting that this might have been the "something." As in Sister 13's case the information did not strike any chords with him, but Philip added,

"I hope that does not mean I will feel I must take over Mike's mission of running the Ladye Park pilgrimage because I just don't feel up to it."

Sister 13 quickly assured him that, if God chooses someone specific to do a job He makes sure the desire and the gifts are given to achieve it. A task which feels a duty or a chore is not a God-given calling, so he Philip should happily sit back and enjoy life, forgetting about the *TROIKA,* although *she* did add that she believed that if he was to become a driving force in the re-establishment of the ancient shrine it was likely to be in connection with his knowledge and gift of Cornish Language speaking. Philip liked that idea and agreed this would certainly not be a duty or a chore but he could not at the time imagine how this would come to fruition.

Easter passed and so did Pentecost with no news as to whether the ESBVM planned by Mike, for June, would still be taking place. Purposely Sister 13 did not make too many enquiries, believing that she would hear news if it was to go ahead, but it was out of her hands if it did not.

On Saturday, 16th June 2001 Sister 13 received a letter from Canon Geach of Truro Cathedral, saying he had taken over organisation of the pilgrimage and it would take place the following Sunday, 24th June, the date originally arranged by Mike Jennings. John and Judith Wilkes, the new owners, were taking the opportunity to have the restored baptistery rededicated by an Anglican minister friend of theirs, in the name of UNITY. Sister 13 was intrigued to hear that it had been restored as she had been unaware of any plans for this and she noted with amusement that the 24th June was the feast day of St John the Baptist, a very suitable day for such a rededication.

She immediately made plans to attend the pilgrimage although as publicity did not seem to have been widespread, Sister 13 surmised that numbers of attendees would be much lower than in previous years and she was correct. She judged the small band, which congregated at 2.30pm on the sunny Sunday at the end of the leafy lane to process the 500 metres to Ladye Park to be about 30 in number. The enthusiasm of the group was evident as they lustily sang out the pilgrim hymns. Even the cows in a field adjoining the route seemed to want to join in, as they rather unmelodiously mooed and charged along on the other side of the hedge.

John and Judith Wilkes had followed with the pilgrims behind the colourful banners, but made their way to the front as the group approached Ladye Park, taking positions at the gate to welcome the walkers into the grounds of their home. Those who had attended previous pilgrimages were immediately aware of something different. There was a sense of openness as a great deal of foliage seemed to have been cut down. The house had been decked with joyful red and gold banners proclaiming "Jesus the King". The most exciting change of all was that the bricked up doorway which had for years been hidden behind a bush, and which Sheila Richards had seen in her 'mystic experience' three years previously, had been opened up and made into an attractive door which was now the main entrance to the house.

Once in the park, the first station was the niche in the remaining wall of what is thought to be the chapel, predating the medieval building, parts of which are built into the present house. The pilgrim banners were ceremoniously placed adjacent to the spot and the local Catholic priest then led the assembled group in the joyful mysteries of the Rosary.

Next station was the ancient well, whose waters were blessed by Canon Geach and then it was over to the baptistery spanning the river, which now had a beautiful corbelled dome. It was here that the assembled group heard from John Wilkes the amazing story of how it came to be rebuilt.

The previous October or November, just a few weeks after John and Judith had moved into Ladye Park there was, in the night, a tremendous storm with thunder and lightning. The Wilkes heard an alarming bang and the next morning, on looking out of their window, they noticed there seemed a large gap in the skyline. On closer investigation it was soon clear that an enormous horse chestnut tree, which must have stood at the entrance to the grounds for hundreds of years, had during the night come crashing to the ground. In falling the trunk had somehow managed to twist itself round in a 45 degree turn to land straight across the old baptistery completely crushing it, but almost miraculously causing no damage to anything else. Surprised at this phenomenon, John Wilkes felt that the fall of the tree was telling him something. Contrary to the usual belief that insurance companies are eager to collect premiums but not so keen to pay out, no difficulties arose with this claim. As a result, a good local stonemason was employed to restore the baptismal edifice. So pleased were the Wilkes with the result, they decided to use the opportunity of having the stonemason and garden specialists on hand to restore other parts of the garden too, although to do this so soon after moving in had not been part of their original plan. The whole restoration had been completed just two weeks before the planned pilgrimage so it was natural to combine the baptistery's rededication to UNITY, with the Ecumenical Society of the Blessed Virgin Mary's celebration.

Finally the group moved over to the pond or lake which some

historians believe could pre-date the baptistery as the site for baptisms. It was immediately apparent that a very attractive small bridge had been erected over a leat, housing the spring which had appeared shortly before the 1999 pilgrimage. One pilgrim, who had attended that pilgrimage when all had drunk of the waters, remarked, examining the new construction, that he would have liked to see a step down, so that it were easier to fill a vessel with water, but another responded by saying that that could possibly come later, the amazing thing was that a feature had been made of the Spring at all, when it was doubtful that the new owners had any idea of its significance or that it had not always been there.

As the clan gathered on the lawn, close to the lake, Canon Geach spoke of past pilgrimages and how the majority of pilgrims, when the shrine of Our Lady of the Park was in its hey day, would have spoken Cornish rather than English. He asked Bard Philip Knight, to say the Lord's Prayer in Cornish, in memory of those who had passed that way in days of yore, and this was followed by the Our Father in the language more commonly understood by the pilgrims of today.

News had recently come to certain members of the group that Philip Knight had produced the text of a draft version of the Mass in Cornish. He had, as a preliminary exercise, translated the English wording in 1997. However, when he sent this translation to Mr R K R Syed MA, an Oxford graduate in Hebrew, Greek and Latin, a practising Anglican and member of the Bishop of Truro's Ecumenical Advisory group for services in Cornish, Mr Syed had replied saying he would be happy to help as checker and adviser, were Philip to embark on a more serious translation of the Mass. This would have to be an accurate translation from the original Latin source, the *Ordo Missae*. Philip Knight rose to the challenge, but he realised a further important requirement was permission from the Bishop of Plymouth, the Right Reverend Christopher Budd, for him to proceed with the project. Bishop Christopher wrote in October 1999 offering him his blessing and saying that Fr Richard Rutt would act as his censor before the translation could be sent to the Vatican for the possible granting of an "Imprimatur".

Philip had set to work and at the time of the 2001 ESBVM Pilgrimage, the draft version, which had been subjected to rigorous checking and amendment was completed. It had been sent to a small number of readers for proof-reading and comment - both linguistic and liturgical and then the final version would be prepared, but both Sister 13 and Pegasus, who was also present at Ladye Park that year, later mentioned separately, the fact that Peggy Pollard had almost prophetically suggested, "One day the Mass will be translated into Cornish." She would, they thought, be delighted that this had happened just five years after her death and in the year which many believe to be the true millennium. They wondered whether her other dream, that the first Cornish Mass should be said in Liskeard would also come true.

To round off the afternoon in true Christian spirit the owners of Ladye Park had nobly invited everyone for tea. Tables and chairs had been set out within view of the now beautifully restored grounds,. As if with some foreknowledge, 27 cups and saucers had been laid up, and there turned out to be exactly 27 pilgrims. Once more Our Lady had shown her planning was impeccable, even if she had as usual delegated to others!

Some pilgrims continued to stroll the grounds either before or after partaking of their refreshment. One remarkable sight was the remains of the fallen chestnut tree sprouting to life. Although the detached trunk and branches had been taken away, the stump and roots had been left and new green leaves were bursting from them. One could not but draw a parallel with images of the Church in the report 'On the Threshold', produced by the Catholic Bishops Conference 2000.

That report cites that geologists tell us that land masses of the earth are plates of continental crust. Sometimes these plates are pulled apart, sometimes one plate dives under another and sometimes two plates slide in opposite directions. Where collisions take place the earth's crust is at its most creative. Mountains are formed, new land is created. The earth is in a continual process of movement and that movement is at its most creative where the earth's crust is at its thinnest and where one plate meets another.

The report points to a conclusion we can draw from this image of the tectonic plates of the earth's crust. First the plates are both solid and flexible. They are secure but also capable of movement. The church too has a solidity and richness of heritage which gives a secure base but it also needs to be flexible.

The report continues by saying we can also draw from our knowledge that new land is only formed where old land dies. The crust of one plate crashes into another, dives under it and disappears. In its place new territory is born. The eternal gospel is always in the process of being reborn. It never dies but the way in which we proclaim it sometimes needs to die in order that new beginnings can happen.

The horse chestnut tree had fallen and crashed into the old baptistery. It was at the point of collision that the stonemason had been able to be at his most creative, building the new corbelled dome over the stream, based on the old, but more suitable for the third millennium, strong enough to withstand not only storms but the tremors of modern day traffic which would pass nearby. The tree, the originator of the change, seemed to be dead. It needed to fall for the change to take place but the roots remain and are putting forth new shoots which will be flexible. They will bend and sway in future winds and storms but they will not be blown away for they are securely based in the solid foundations of the original tree. So too the Church. Many feel it is "dead" for them. This should not be looked at entirely negatively. Perhaps God is calling us to look for the positive, to see where new territory has been or is being formed and to realise that the new shoots are to enable it to continue to grow and develop for the next thousand years.

Driftwood showing carved Madonna and child, found on St Agnes'
Beach. Photo taken in local art gallery, where it is now on display.

214

Chaptra Peswardhek

(Chapter Fourteen)

Bora nowydh an skrifer rag an Grerva Gellys
Author's new dawn for the lost shrine

As we stand at the brink of the third millennium and the threshold of a new era, there is a question, which comes to mind: "What of the future for the lost Shrine of Liskeard?"

If, as many believe Our Lady expressed a wish in 1955 to be brought back to Liskeard, it would appear from recent events, that the time is drawing very close for her wish to be fulfilled. Why there has been such a time lapse between her request to return and its fulfilment we will never know. We can only surmise. Similarly we can only guess as to the way the plan will unfurl in the future. We can be sure of one thing: that it is unlikely to be as we imagine it will be, for the future never is. However, there is no harm in dreaming and sometimes dreams become reality. Strangely enough, David Whittley, at the beginning of the year 2001 had a dream relating to this subject. He is not a believer in dreams other than that they are the working of the subconscious, but this particular dream was vivid enough for him to remember it clearly and then to relate it to me.

In his dream he was in a large grassy area, which he took to be Ladye Park, although he had never been there. All around him a crowd of people was milling, waiting for something to happen. In the middle of the lawn was a Cornish round house, similar to the one he had painted on his Pig Meadow Lane Mural and in the painting 'Return to Ladye Park.' He was standing next to this house, which he believed to be a chapel and which was bathed in light. It was open on all sides and a stone altar had been placed inside. He was aware in his dream, that he had been commissioned to paint the domed ceiling. He did not know what he had painted but he could see celestial figures in the centre. Just then an elderly professor-type gentleman with spectacles and a beard came up to him and congratulated him on his fresco, telling him that the "Four winds" he had painted coming from four corners of the dome (he was not aware he had painted them) represented the four great religions of the world, which would all come on pilgrimage to Liskeard, and there the dream ended. He had no idea which beliefs were considered the "four great religions."

Though this dream could mean anything or nothing, I have to admit it set me thinking.

In 1979 the shrine of Our Lady of the Park, Liskeard, was dedicated as a shrine for "Unity". This was at a time when inter-religious dialogue had newly been recognised by Christians as an important element in the way ahead. On the whole, however, this went unnoticed by the general laity who were aware mainly of ecumenical relations between different Christian denominations. Maybe, one of the reasons Our Lady only sowed the seeds of her return and did not intervene to allow them to blossom too soon was that she was waiting for a time when a common witness to shared values could extend far beyond the Christian churches.

The greatest example in the twentieth century of this type of shared witness took place on October 27th 1986, the World Day of Prayer for Peace. On that day representatives of twelve religions including the Dalai Lama, the Chief Rabbi of Rome, the Archbishop of Canterbury and the Pope all came together in Assisi, the home of St Francis, well known for his humble love of friends, enemies and the poor, as well as birds, animals and all God's creation. With incense, water, fire, flowers, song, dance, drums and other instruments, the assembled group witnessed to their belief in the primacy of the spiritual, the preservation of Mother earth, international justice and world peace.

Without suppressing their real differences, all were united by these common goals and aspirations. Perhaps without knowing it the re-hallowing of the Lost Shrine in 1979 and the dedication to unity were a preparation for a new role for Liskeard in the 21st century: to revitalise our response to the Gospel in a spirit of openness to humanity's wide ranging search for knowledge of the mystery of existence. In the document Nostra Aetate (Our Time) from the Second Vatican Council, it is stated:

"Men look to their different religions for an answer to the unsolved riddles of human existence" and "throughout history, even to the present day, there is found among different peoples a certain awareness of a hidden power, which lies behind the course of nature and the events of human life."

My dream is that Our Lady's return to the Lost Shrine will act as a magnet not only for Christians but for others too. Her presence would welcome all belonging to religious traditions which respect the dignity of the human being and the sanctity of life, as well as those who, though not part of any established religion, are searching for the meaning of life. And perhaps, through Our Lady's help, they might come to find the answers they seek, for as Christ said, "Ask and you will receive. Seek and you will find."

Just as Christ was born into a Jewish culture, but His Church moved into a dominantly Roman one, so now it is moving into a global culture, with the introduction of the internet, ease of travel and communication. The Church must, then, address itself to this global culture and set a clear example of how to participate in it. One way in which the Church can do this is by explaining its moral and ethical teachings in the context of the Natural Law, a law which is written on the hearts of every human being, of whatever religion. It is this time-honoured Catholic understanding of the Natural Law which makes it essential for us to respect and value the diversity of human spiritual endeavour, whilst holding fast to the truths that have been revealed through Christ.

When Pope John Paul II was asked why there were so many religions, he replied, "You speak of many religions. Instead I will attempt to show the common fundamental element and the common root of these religions ... Instead of marvelling at the fact that providence allows such a great variety of religions, we should be amazed at the number of common elements found within them." Here, the Pope is speaking of that deep awareness of the Natural Law that is part of every human life, and pushes us all to seek closer union with God. It is this spiritual awareness that prompts man's religious search, if he is in earnest, even when he does not hold to revealed religious truth.

I believe that just as Assisi represented for the gathering of world religious leaders in 1986 the ideals of St Francis, with which they were all able to identify, so I believe Liskeard could become the spot where Mary the Mother of God could be cherished as an icon of motherhood. Every human has had a mother and can identify with one. The perfect mother cares for her children, loves them, builds a home for them where they grow and learn; she will never desert them, no matter what they do. She continually strives for peace and harmony in her family. As a result her children love her in return and want to be with her. And Mary whispers softly to those who listen to her, those words she spoke to the servants at the marriage feast at Cana: "Do whatever He tells you."

Cornwall has everything that is needed for such a pilgrimage site, from rough seas pounding powerfully over rocks and peaceful countryside, to mysterious standing stones, remnants of ancient religions which thousands of years ago celebrated the mysteries which lay behind the façade of mundane life. Holy wells and churches abound for those who who value links with early Christians.

For religious and secular alike, a visit to the Eden project near St Austell with its myriad plants and trees from all over the world cannot but stir a feeling of wonder and awe in an enquiring mind. Here, all are united in acknowledging the mystery of creation.

Catholics attending Holy Mass could enjoy the proposed mural, which will be an icon, produced as an aid to meditation. For as William Johnson says in his book 'Arise My Love - Mysticism for a new Era' (Apr 2000), "The icon, unlike the idol, is a window to the divine. It leads to deep and imageless contemplative experience."

In nearby Gunnislake a World Peace 2000 Project has been established. A beautiful scented hybrid yellow tea rose was bred for the purpose and thousands of them were planted by communities throughout England, Scotland, Ireland and Wales in dedication to World Peace in November 2000. A follow-on from this has been the development of a World Peace Garden stained-glass window, crafted by the monks of Buckfast Abbey. It is a single design that depicts the universe in miniature with the rising sun, the moon, the earth, the stars, the sky, the sea and a rainbow, laid out within a circular boundary. In the heart of the garden is a living flame, representing the spark of light within everyone - that law which is written on all our hearts, irrespective of religious, cultural or political differences.

Perhaps the rose and the window could be combined to create a focal point to pray for unity and global peace. The rose has always been a flower connected with Mary, and 'Our Lady Queen of Peace' is said to be one of her favourite titles, so what could be more fitting to mark the return of Our Lady to Liskeard? Only time itself, as with everything, will reveal any Divine plan, if there is one, for the Lost Shrine of Liskeard. Meanwhile we would do well to meditate on the poem written below in Cornish. I make no value judgement about it, but simply include it here as part of the strange and wonderful chain of events and coincidences associated with our Lady's lost shrine of Liskeard. It was found in manuscript form at a convent in the New Forest in August 2000. So far no-one has been able to discover whose work it is or how it came to be there.

Ha ni ow tos nes
Dhe gen pobel
Dhe gen gonisogeth
Dhe gen kryjyans
Agan kynsa ober
Yw diwiska agan eskisyow
Rag bos SANS an tyller
Mayth eson ow tos nes dhodho
Poken ni a omwel martesen
Ow stankya war hunros ken onan
Poessa hwath
Martesen ni a wra ankevi
Bos Dyw ena
Kyns agan devedhyans ni

THE LOST SHRINE OF LISKEARD

Our First Task
In approaching
Another people
Another culture
Another religion
Is to take off our shoes
For the place
We are approaching
is HOLY
Else we may find ourselves
Treading on Another's dream
More serious still
We may forget
That God was there
Before our arrival.

Appendix

Ballade to Michael by Margaret Pollard

You are so conscious of your dreadful powers
The regular laugh on a deep dimple runs
The brow portcullis lifts and lowers above your eyes
Those lustrous onyx suns that have the might of armour piercing
guns
That shoot to kill and hover the Tare Plane and breach the Tenant
Trace and bastions
But that's not love
Or is it Michael Maine?

Such pious looks invading Adele's Bower
Count Ory and his men disguised as nuns might have put on
The plush like peony flowers, the smile that would dissolve the
hearts of Huns
God, not a ring of towers like Carcasson can shield
The too impressionable brain against the beauty that distracts and
stuns
But that's not love
Or is it Michael Maine?

Though I could sit and stare at you for hours
A mind well disciplined emotion shuns
And I well trained look sidelong not devours
Hard flippancy mounts guard with jests and puns
Passions, wode biting bears, are tamed with buns
And everyone may guess and guess in vain
Save God who hears my private orisms
But that's not love
Or is it Michael Maine?

Prince, Your caprices are most maddening ones
Your moods and whims would drive a saint insane
The pressure can be measured up in tons
But that's not love
Or is it Michael Maine?

Margaret Pollard wrote many more poems and ditties, but they were usually humorous ones, which she said she wrote to make people (particularly her husband, Pollard) laugh and if they did not laugh she tore them up and wrote another. One such ditty was:

<u>*The Song of Mrs. Waring*</u>
My name's Betsy Waring
I goes out a - charing,
And after my work I gets paid half a crown:
I gets the rheumatics
Which comes of damp attics
And your pair o'stairs to go up and down-
And I often hears rumours
Of wars and contumours
And earthquakes, and comics as lights up the sky:
Steam ninjins a-bustin!
And banks as folks trust in -
But they don't never fret an old 'woman like I!

In October 1973 she was interviewed for a small newspaper printed locally at the time, entitled "Peninsular West." Though she did not keep a copy of the article herself a friend did. An extract is printed below. Unfortunately extensive enquiries have failed to identify either the journalist or editors of the paper.

<u>*Profile Of Margaret Pollard from 'Peninsular West' Wednesday 24th October 1973*</u>
Mrs Margaret Pollard, self confessed hermit of Truro and lover of "Gods, mythology and all that"; strides energetically about her room with the words, "Big Sister" emblazoned in Chinese across her smock. For a woman who has spent most of her activities in pursuit if the 'inner life' and has now embarked on what promises to be the longest tapestry in the world, the title is somewhat apt.

The tapestry threatens to grow to a length of 360 feet (some 20 feet is already finished) and has been 'commissioned' by Michael Maine, "a very, very remarkable boy indeed" who inspired Mrs Pollard with the idea of basing the tapestry on the Narnia books of C.S. Lewis, featuring Aslan the lion.

Michael Maine is an accomplished organist and the possessor of a fertile imagination which Mrs Pollard gains endless pleasure" in translating into action. She admits to being a kind of "army transport mule - if I'm given a job to do I can do it, but I'm not very good at originating ideas." The Narnia tapestry is just one of several that drape themselves with worklike abandon around the room, which in turn is filled with books, pictures and writings, many of which are pinned or written directly onto the walls.

Mrs Pollard has a great regard for the 'quote' which act as signposts, not to say milestones in her religious and literary life and if the right one is not actually on the walls then Mrs Pollard has the facility for instant recall in order to qualify any given point of view. The fact that they contradict each other is neither here nor there since "the human mind is capable of accommodating simultaneously an extraordinary number of contradictions" and if some of them appear a little obscure then "no man can explain himself or can get himself explained."

Mrs Pollard delights in conversation but concurs with GB Shaw that the "ideal love affair is one conducted by post." indeed Mrs Pollard is an avid correspondent to friends in all corners of the world, and writes and translates in both Russian and German. All her amusements remain solitary ones with no regrets about her insular way of life. "It's been great fun and it's getting better all the time", she says, "if I'm not writing, I'm making tapestries here in my mini-factory."

The latest addition to the 'mini-factory' is a tapestry based on a painting by Hieronymous Bosch, The Creation of the World, also suggested by Michael Maine. Mrs Pollard is not quite sure how she will treat the centre section filled with Bosch-like fantasies, but "when I get on to the angels I'll be alright."

1991 MARIA WYNN A GERNOW

ILOW HA GERYOW
GANS PHILIP KNIGHT

Hymn to Our Lady in the Park
by Dr Margaret Pollard

Details from the tapestry of the Coronation of
Our Lady, surrounded by the Fourteen Holy Helpers.

227

David Whittley's "Return to Ladye Park" (oil of canvas, 1988)

"La Vierge à la Porcelaine" painted by Margaret Pollard.

230   Two of the six Celtic crosses erected by different Christian communities in Liskeard to mark the Jubilee Year 2000. And below: in another
example of ecumenical co-operation, pilrgims pray the Our Father
together in Cornish at Ladye Park, June 2001.

The newly restored gardens at Ladye Park, June, 2001. In the background can be seen the restored baptistry and in the foreground the leat for the spring which appeared in 1999.

232   Above: Kerrid's *Well of Eternal Youth*.
And a view of Ladye Park from the top of the Mass Path.

Above: Philip Knight (left) singing *Maria, Wynn a Gernow* at the Pan Celtic
Festival in Galway, accompnaied by Michael Jennings, 1992.

Below: Ladye Park House decorated with banners
for the pilgrimage, June 2001

Shining out amongst other flowers in a Cornish garden,
a *Peace Rose 2000*, planted November 2000.